SPAIN

Ramón J. Sender

(TWAS 307)

RAMÓN J. SENDER

Ramón J. Sender

By CHARLES L. KING
University of Colorado

Twayne Publishers, Inc. :: New York

Copyright © 1974 by Twayne Publishers, Inc.

All Rights Reserved

Library of Congress Cataloging in Publication Data

King, Charles L
   Ramón J. Sender.

   (Twayne's world authors series, TWAS 307. Spain)
   Bibliography: p.
   1. Sender, Ramón José, 1901–
QP6635.E65Z7   863'.6'2   73–19612
ISBN 0–8057–2815–5

To Eileen, Gail, Carol, and Laura

Preface

Ramón Sender's preeminence among living Spanish novelists is widely recognized by critics of Spanish literature. Some, for example, Marcelino C. Peñuelas, place him "at the head of Spanish novelists of our time," and by that statement, Peñuelas is careful to point out, he means to rate Sender above Pío Baroja, the celebrated Basque novelist (1872–1956) who is usually regarded as Spain's greatest novelist of this century.[1] My aim here is to present for English readers as comprehensive a picture of this author as may be permitted in the space available; he is to be considered primarily as a novelist, but also as a relatively prolific writer of short stories, theater, poetry, essays, and journalistics works. It must be kept in mind that even as these words are being typed, Sender (b. 1901), still vigorous and strong of will, is at his desk in California continuing his yet unfinished literary work; indeed, he has just submitted for publication the manuscript of a major new novel which will probably see print before this book. Will the new novel surpass in artistic quality and depth of vision all previous Senderian works? *¿Quién sabe?* as the Spanish peasant sometimes says, shrugging his shoulders. Only time will tell.

Since so little information on Sender's life has thus far been published, Chapter I is a short but accurate biographical sketch. In Chapter 2 I have sought to relate the major ideological and literary currents of this century to the author's work. Writing an adequate critical-analytical survey of all of Sender's vast and diverse literary production (thirty-one novels, eight books of short stories, four of theater, one of poetry, and thirteen of essays and journalism, in a count which eliminates all duplications) in one book is, of course, impossible. It has obviously been necessary to choose for special treatment only a few works, and to give only minimal consideration to his many remaining books. I selected for greatest attention two novels, *The Sphere* and *The King and the Queen*, devoting a chapter to each; to the first because it is the author's most ambitious philosophical work, and to the second because it is highly representative of the novelist at his artistic and philosophical best. In three other chapters I discuss each of Sender's remaining novels, following a chronological order, and devoting special attention to the more significant works and less to those which I regard as "minor" or relatively unimportant to an understanding of the author's total production. In order not to leave with the reader the false impression that Sender is only a novelist (although he is that primarily), I have condensed into one chapter a brief discussion of his many books of short stories, theatrical works, poetry, essays, and journalism. Hopefully this book will serve to suggest areas for fruitful Senderian criticism in the future. Except where otherwise indicated, all translations are mine.

My sincere appreciation goes to the American Philosophical Society and to the Council on Research and Creative Work of the University of Colorado for their grants-in-aid which have facilitated the preparation of this study. I wish also to acknowledge the courtesy of the editors and publishers of *The American Book Collector*, *Books Abroad*, *Hispania*, and *PMLA* for permission to reuse short excerpts from material I have published in these journals.

CHARLES L. KING

University of Colorado

Contents

Chronology

1901 February 3: Ramón José Sender Garcés is born in Chalamera de Cinca, Province of Huesca, in Aragon.

1902 Sender family returns to Alcolea de Cinca, a town eight kilometers from Chalamera (from which the Senders had moved to Chalamera about two years previously).

1911 Family moves to Tauste, northwest of Zaragoza in Aragon.

1912 June 17: Ramón passes entrance examinations for the Institute of Zaragoza.

1913– Attends a boarding school in Reus, the Colegio de San
1914 Ildefonso.

1914 Family moves to Zaragoza.

1914– Ramón studies at the Institute of Zaragoza. Wins first prize
1917 in a short story contest sponsored by the *Heraldo de Aragón,* the newspaper of Zaragoza.

1917 Family moves to Caspe; Sender to Alcañiz where he works as a pharmacy clerk while continuing his work toward his *bachillerato* (high school diploma) by taking examinations in courses from the Colegio de los Padres Escolapios of Alcañiz and transferring the credit to the Institute of Teruel.

1918 Ramón receives the *bachillerato* from the Institute of Teruel. Enrolls in the Law School of the University of Madrid, but soon leaves Madrid to join family which moved during the the year to Huesca.

1918– Acts as editor of *La Tierra,* a small rural newspaper published
1921 in Huesca.

1921– Attends Law School of the University of Madrid and works
1922 as a pharmacist's assistant in Madrid.

1923– Serves for fourteen months in the Regiment of Asturias, with
1924 action in the African campaign.

1924 Joins the editorial staff of *El Sol,* liberal newspaper in Madrid.

1927 Imprisoned for three months in the Cárcel Modelo (Model Jail) in Madrid for alleged participation in revolutionary activities. Freed upon the insistence of the Press Association of Madrid.

1928 Ramón publishes his first book, *El problema religioso en Méjico (The Religious Problem in Mexico).*

1930   Publishes his first novel, *Imán* (*Pro Patria*), an antiwar work based on his experiences in the Moroccan War. Resigns from *El Sol* to devote full time to freelance journalism and to the writing of novels.

1932   Publishes the novel *Siete domingos rojos* (*Seven Red Sundays*).

1934   Marries Amparo Barayón. Visits the Soviet Union.

1936   July 18: Spanish Civil War begins. Sender enlists in the Republican forces. Execution of his wife and his brother by the Nationalist forces.

1938   Visits the United States on a speaking mission for the Spanish government. Goes to France in December.

1939   Settles in Mexico City.

1942   Having received a Guggenheim Fellowship, Sender emigrates to the United States.

1943   August 12: Marries Florence Hall, a citizen of the United States.

1943–   Lectures at the University of Denver, the University of Colo-
1944   rado, and Harvard University.

1944–   Professor of Spanish literature at Amherst College (Massa-
1945   chusetts).

1946   Becomes a naturalized citizen of the United States.

1947–   Professor of Spanish Literature at the University of New
1963   Mexico. Publishes many books, including the novels *La esfera* (*The Sphere*), *El rey y la reina* (*The King and the Queen*), *and Réquiem por un campesino español* (*Requiem for a Spanish Peasant*) during this period.

1963   Divorces Florence Hall. Visits France. Moves to the Los Angeles area in California.

1965–   Visiting professor of Spanish Literature at the University of
1971   Southern California.

1971–   Lives in San Diego, California, where he continues to write.

CHAPTER 1

Biography

IN June of 1969 I had four interviews with Ramón Sender in his apartment bordering the campus of the University of Southern California, where from February of 1965 until June, 1971, he was Visiting Professor of Spanish Literature. I had gone to Los Angeles with the hope that the author would provide me with adequate information for a full-scale biography. But my hope was not to be realized! The very idea of a biography, of something completed and therefore "dead," seemed to repel him. How I still remember his emphatic words, "My life is not over yet, far from it!" In the next three years Sender published four new novels and a book of short stories! One of the novels, *En la vida de Ignacio Morel* (*In the Life of Ignacio Morel*), won for him the Planeta Prize for 1969, Spain's most lucrative, if not most prestigious, literary prize. He was right, his work was not finished, nor is it at this writing (April, 1973). Don Ramón continues today his prolific literary production. As for biography, he points out that his "life"—his inner or essential biography—is in his works, there for all who are interested to see.

Yet, though we grant that Sender's subjective reality or "essential biography" revealed in his vast literary production is what really makes him interesting and important to us, I must insist that, for that very reason, an accurate account of the external events of his life cannot fail to interest his readers. I, however, must leave to others the writing of a more complete Senderian biography; in this book I include only those data which I judge to be most significant or helpful in interpreting the author's work.

Since Don Ramón is such a highly autobiographic author, Josefa Rivas tried briefly to reconstruct his life from his writings alone.[1] For her effort to have succeeded, she would first have

13

had to determine which literary characters are actually auto-biographical; secondly, she would have had to know which conditions and events in each character's "life" were true to Sender's life, and which were not. It then would have been necessary to have each detail verified by Sender, in which case it would have been more efficient simply to have gotten the information directly from the author in the first place. A trust-worthy Senderian biography cannot be reconstructed from the corpus of the author's work.

It does not seem likely to me that Sender will ever write a fully factual account of his life nor that he will collaborate adequately with anyone wishing to write his biography. Though he is a writer of great integrity and sincerity, he has always managed to shroud his own life with a sense of mystery, knowing as he does the attraction of mystery. In the prologue to his novel, *Los cinco libros de Ariadna* (*The Five Books of Ariadne*), which is admittedly highly autobiographical in content, he writes: "The truth is that each time I realize that someone is trying to define me I use every means to make it difficult for him. It is known that he who knows us limits us, he who understands us dominates us, he who defines us kills us."[2] Rafael Sender, the author's youngest brother, told me in a conversation (in Barcelona in 1969) that Sender had always sought to protect his inner life from the prying eyes of others; he spoke of Sender's strong sense of *pudor* or modesty, a shy sense of decorum that fears that people might penetrate too deeply into his inner self or motives, and thus acquire some sort of "control" over him. When he senses that somebody is getting too close to understanding him he will, says Don Rafael, deliberately try to mislead and confuse that person. "He who knows you destroys you," a maxim by Baltasar Gracián, a seventeenth-century writer and fellow Aragonese, has weighed heavily with Sender.

I *Aragonese Beginnings, 1901–1921*

In a biographical note written for the editors of *Twentieth Century Authors,* Sender states: "They tell me I was born in 1902. I do not believe it. My impression is that I have lived always, and I remember with more clarity, for example, medieval Spanish scenes than episodes of my childhood or youth."[3] Later he explains that "because I am out of tune with the affairs, the people, and the customs of my time, I have that feeling I have mentioned, of never having been born, and that other notion (which is the same at base and inseparable from it) of not dying. This has nothing to do with academic ideas. It is a biological feeling."[4] Regardless of Sender's "biological feeling" of "never having been born" and of what "they" told him, accuracy demands that we record here that he was born on February 3, 1901, in the village of Chalamera de Cinca, of the province of Huesca in Aragon, and not in 1902 in Alcolea de Cinca as erroneously reported in several publications.[5]

At the time of Sender's birth his father, José Sender, was serving as town clerk (*Secretario de Ayuntamiento*) for both Chalamera de Cinca and Alcolea de Cinca. The latter was a town of about 2,500 inhabitants in 1901 (now about 1,700) eight kilometers from Chalamera. Not only both of Sender's parents, but also three of his four grandparents were born in Alcolea.

Sender's mother, Andresa Garcés Laspalas, taught school in Chalamera for one or two years, including the year in which the future novelist was born. In fact, the Senders had moved from Alcolea to Chalamera so that she could teach there without the long ride that would have been necessary had they continued to live in Alcolea. Her first son, José Lázaro Eugenio Sender y Garcés, born September 6, 1899, had died in infancy: Thus Ramón, being the oldest surviving male son, was the family "heir," according to Spanish tradition. In all, Sender's mother gave birth to nineteen children, of which only ten—five of each sex—survived to adulthood. Her first child, Concha, for many years has lived in Madrid where she recently became a widow. A younger daughter, Carmen, has for years taught literature at the Goya Institute in Zaragoza. Sender has shown a lifelong respect and affection for his mother; it is significant that José, the hero of his three-volume, autobiographical novel, *Crónica del alba* (*Chronicle of Dawn*), has the surname of Garcés.

In 1902 Sender's family returned to Alcolea de Cinca where

father Sender continued to serve as town clerk until about 1911. The action of *El lugar de un hombre* (*A Man's Place*) occurs in and around Alcolea; in fact, in its opening pages there is a description of the town, clearly identifiable as Alcolea.[6]

Alcolea is in a rich agricultural region, and young Ramón was free outside of school hours to play in the orchards, truck gardens, and groves which encroach upon the town from the rich river bottom opposite the cliff overhanging the town. It would be reasonable to assume that the boy Sender, as he relates in *A Man's Place*, spent many days helping his paternal grandfather on his farm nearby. There is no evidence that his father himself had a farm here.[7] The Senders owned a home facing onto the town square, only a few yards from the town hall and directly across from the Catholic church, the church alluded to in *A Man's Place*. The Sender home, which today bears the address of 2 Travesía de Santa Cruz, was sold in 1922 or 1923 to Antonio Sierra, who with his family was still occupying it when I visited the Sierra family there in August of 1969.

Antonio Sierra as a young boy knew the Sender family quite well, and was a good friend of Manuel, one of Sender's younger brothers, who, while mayor of Huesca, was executed at the outbreak of the Civil War by the Nationalists. Mr. Sierra's comments to me on Sender are worth recording here (my English translation):

Young Ramón was completely different from his father. His father was a religious fanatic, and from a very early age the son rebelled against religious practice. Sender's father was very strict; his sons were disciplined almost like soldiers as they sat around the family table for meals; his boys were never nursing babies.

There was an absolute incompatibility between Ramón and his father. Both were of strong character, both intransigent. This incompatibility has determined the son's attitude, pushing him to an opposing viewpoint. For example, the religious severity of his father (who imposed upon him from the cradle on all kinds of religious duties) led Ramón to violent reaction against all such imposed religious duties.

Sender's father was very intelligent. Also the son.

In 1911 or 1912 the Sender family moved to Tauste where José Sender had accepted another position as town clerk. Nothing specific is known about this time in Tauste except that Ramón there passed his entrance examinations into the Institute of Zaragoza on June 17, 1912. It appears that through a school in Tauste (recognized by the Institute of Zaragoza) he was able to begin his work toward the high school degree while remaining at home. His transcript at the Institute of Teruel (to which he later transferred) shows that he received the grade of good (*notable*) for courses in Latin, Spanish Geography, and Arithmetic from the Institute of Zaragoza during the academic year, 1912–13. Some of the adventures in *Chronicle of Dawn* occurred in a castle, clearly identifiable as the castle of Sancho Garcés near Tauste, where the Sender family spent summer vacations.

I can only speculate that it was the conflict between father and son that led the father to send Ramón to a boarding school, the Colegio de San Ildefonso managed by the Hermanos de la Sagrada Familia (Brothers of the Sacred Family) in Reus, near Tarragona in Catalonia, for the academic year of 1913–14. Sender was twelve when he entered this school.

Before the academic year in Reus had finished, Sender's family had moved to Zaragoza, living first to the side of the Audiencia (court house) at the corner of Galliponti Street and later moving to Don Juan de Aragón Street. Sender's father was now directing an insurance business. Upon the conclusion of the academic year in Reus Ramón joined his family in Zaragoza, and for the next three years (1914–1917) he attended the Institute of Zaragoza. It was while a student at the Institute that he began demonstrating his literary talent. At the age of fifteen or sixteen he won first prize in a short story writing contest sponsored by the *Heraldo de Aragón* (*Herald of Aragon*), one of Spain's oldest newspapers and which is still published in the Aragonese capital; later the journal *Lecturas* (*Readings*) in Barcelona published his novelette, "Una hoguera en la noche" ("A Bonfire at Night"), as winner of first prize in a short novel writing contest. According to Sender's brother, Rafael, Ramón was seventeen or eighteen years old at the time. While at the Institute of Zaragoza Sender founded and published a weekly student literary journal, *El Cinquito* (*The Little Five*), so named because it was sold for five centavos.

Father Sender's insurance business in Zaragoza began to fail

toward 1917; its success apparently depended on the victory
of the Germans in the War. In 1917 the Sender family once
again moved, this time to Caspe in southern Aragon where
José Sender had been offered his familiar position of town
clerk. Ramón, however, did not accompany his family to Caspe,
but went to Alcañiz, another Aragonese town, where he supported
himself by working as a pharmacy clerk.

While working in Alcañiz, Ramón arranged to transfer credits
from the Institute of Zaragoza to the Institute of Teruel and to
continue his studies toward his high school diploma by taking
examinations in the remaining required courses from the Colegio
de los Padres Escolapios de Alcañiz, accredited by the Institute
of Teruel (Instituto Nacional de Enseñanza Media de Teruel)
for this purpose. Having passed the required examinations,
Sender was granted his bachelor's degree from the Institute
of Teruel in the spring of 1918.[8]

Sender's file in the Institute of Teruel (file number 5122)
which I examined reveals that the future novelist was not a
model student; with few exceptions, his grade was merely
aprobado (passing); he received the grade of *notable* (good)
in Latin, Geography of Spain, Arithmetic, History of Spain,
and in the first and second courses of Drawing (*Dibujo*); the
only course in which he received the grade of excellent
(*sobresaliente*) in the ordinary examinations was in Universal
History, taken at the Institute of Zaragoza during the year of
1914–1915; in the extraordinary examination for Arithmetic-
Geometry (*Nociones y ejercicios de Aritmética y Geometría*),
he received the grade of excellent. Having failed Agriculture
and General Chemistry in 1916–1917 at the Institute of Zaragoza,
he repeated these courses with the Padres Escolapios in Alcañiz
in order to achieve passing grades in them.

Upon graduation from the Institute of Teruel, Sender went
directly to Madrid where he enrolled in the Law School of the
Central University of Madrid. In an interview with the author
by José Luis Salado, editor of the *Heraldo de Madrid* (*Herald
of Madrid*), in 1969, Sender, speaking of this time in his life, said:

They wanted me to become a lawyer, and it is to the Ateneo
(Atheneum) that I owe the fact that they did not get their way.

Here I received the first direct and deep impression of a Spanish reality totally different from what had been presented to me. I read in a disorderly manner, voraciously and naturally; I also wrote. At that age it is inevitable; but as I lacked an intellectualist vanity those writings had a simple and sentimental air, and were quite tolerable. So, a poem dedicated to Rosa Luxemburg on the first anniversary of her assassination came out in *El País* [*The Nation*, a Madrilian newspaper] with all honors and gained for me certain admonitions. I was a minor of age—seventeen—and I had to return to the province. There I worked on a newspaper. A regional writer now dead used to say: "Journalist in Huesca, chauffeur in Santolarieta [district in Madrid]."[9]

About the time that Sender was beginning his law courses (although obviously his true interest was to become a writer) his family moved from Caspe to the provincial capital of Huesca. There his father had taken a position as administrator of the agricultural property of the Duke of Solferino at Almuniente; at about the same time he assumed management of a small rural newspaper, *La Tierra* (*The Land*), published in Huesca by the Association of Farmers and Ranchers of Upper Aragon.[10] After only a short stay in Madrid young Sender was called to join his family in Huesca, where for the next three years he acted—although unofficially—as editor of *La Tierra*.

II *Student, Soldier, and Journalist, 1921–1930*

In 1921 Sender left Huesca and *La Tierra* to return to Madrid where for a time he worked as an assistant to a pharmacist while renewing his work at the University. He never graduated from Law School; indeed, the only university degree that he has ever received was an honorary Doctorate in Letters granted to him by the University of New Mexico in June of 1968. In 1923 he was drafted for service with the Army. The ill-managed, ill-starred, so-called "War of Reconquest" in Morocco was being waged by Spain, a nation which was still reeling from the defeat suffered at Annual two years earlier at the hands of the Moorish chieftain, Abd el Krim, and his Riff tribesmen. Entering as a private, Ramón rapidly ascended the military ranks by taking the official examinations for promotion every three months. After the first three months he was promoted to *cabo* (corporal); three months later to *sargento* (sergeant); then to *sub-oficial* (warrant officer); and finally to *alférez* (second lieutenant), the highest nonprofessional rank possible and the rank held by Sender upon his discharge after fourteen months of service.[11] He saw action in the African campaign, an experience which forms the basis for his first novel, *Imán* (*Magnet*, but published in English as *Earmarked for Hell* in England, and as *Pro Patria* in the United States), 1930. Attached to the Regiment of Asturias, known as the Regimiento Ceriñola 42, he was cited for bravery in action and was awarded the Medal of Morocco.

Upon military discharge in 1924, the young veteran joined the editorial staff of *El Sol* (*The Sun*), the most prestigious liberal newspaper in Madrid of the twenties. The story has circulated that for many years there was an ink blotch on the wall of one of the editorial offices of *El Sol*, left there when the fiery young journalist threw a bottle of ink at one of his colleagues in the midst of a debate.[12]

In 1928, having been encouraged by a group of his friends, Sender collected articles which he had written for *El Sol* and published them together as his first book, *El problema religioso en Méjico* (*The Religious Problem in Mexico*), a study of the relations of Church and State in Mexico. The Prologue was signed by Ramón del Valle-Inclán. The book was well received and won recognition for Sender as an intelligent observer of the problems of Spanish-American countries as well as the position of secretary of the Ibero-American section of the Ateneo, the prestigious literary club of Madrid.

During these years Sender began his close and lasting friendship with that colorful personage and superb stylist, Valle-Inclán. His admiration for the great Galician author has been evident in many articles, and especially in his book, *Valle-Inclán y la dificultad de la tragedia* (*Valle-Inclán and the Difficulty of Tragedy*), 1965. The young Aragonese writer also came to know personally most of the other members of the Generation of 1898, including Miguel de Unamuno for whom he acquired a persistent antipathy which he has expressed on numerous occasions through the years.

From childhood on Sender has been a rebel against the *status quo*: at first his rebellion took the form of antagonism toward his father, soon it extended to a distrust of the adult world in general, and later to an attitude of social protest. The conflict with his father was deep and no doubt marked him for life. Andrea Sender, the author's daughter, once told me that as a child she was aware of the deep rift between her father and grandfather Sender. The author's younger brother, Rafael, confirmed this lifelong antipathy between father and son. I have already quoted Antonio Sierra's statement that between father and son there was "an absolute incompatibility"; in Sierra's opinion, this conflict has been of determinative influence in Sender's life. A Catalonian psychiatrist, Jaime Lluis y Navas, in an article, "Los sentimientos edípicos en la novelística de Ramón Sender" ("Oedipal Sentiments in the Novels of Ramón Sender"),[13] seeks to find the root of Sender's sociopolitical rebellion in his unhappy relations with his father. It seems reasonable to assume that the author's early difficulties with his father have conditioned his attitude toward society, and especially toward the authoritarianism of the Roman Catholic Church in Spain. References to the son-father conflict persist in Sender's work long after José Sender had died.[14]

Apart from several minor acts of rebellion in his early youth referred to in his fiction (but none of which is documented), it is clear that Sender in 1927, at the age of twenty-six, was arrested and imprisoned for alleged participation in revolutionary agitation against the dictatorship of Primo de Rivera. Held without trial for three months in the Cárcel Modelo (Model Jail) in Madrid, he was freed upon the insistence of the Press Association of Madrid. Sender's attitude is obviously that of the Journalist, the protagonist of *Orden público (Public Order),* 1931, his second novel. In jail the Journalist meditates: "History is the fear of men to tread new ground, to advance one foot. They hang onto the past as women hang onto the home of their parents. ... Let us also sweep away history. I want to be the sweeper of historical facts and ideas, the disinfectant of old and dusty consciences, the mover and activator of the new Spain."[15] Sender's quixotic opposition to oppression, wherever he finds it, is a constant in all of his life and work; it is well expressed in this early work: "The case was—thought the Journalist—not to be silent, not to tolerate, scandalously to accuse injustice, to make of individual and collective life an uninterrupted protest which perforce everybody would have to hear."[16]

III   Novelist and Journalistic Writer, 1930–1936

Sender's first novel, Imán, took its title, which means "magnet," from its protagonist, Viance, because he "attracted iron—in other words, misfortune, violence." An immediate success, the novel was reprinted in an inexpensive popular edition in Spain in 1933 which sold thirty thousand copies, and within a few years had been translated into the following languages: German, Dutch, Portuguése, English, Polish, Russian, Hebrew, White Russian, Ukrainian, Chinese, and fragmentarily into French. Its German translation exhausted its thirty thousand copies in less than a year, and "not without provoking enthusiastic commentary among the most prestigious critics who said that the work contributed more elements for the psychic and biological study of war."[17]

Encouraged by the brilliant success of Pro Patria (Imán's American title), Sender at the age of twenty-nine abandoned El Sol in 1930 to devote himself wholly to the writing of novels and journalistic articles. During the next few years he was indeed busy; I found 185 articles, almost all of them lengthy, in the Madrilian newspaper, La Libertad (Liberty), signed by Sender during the period 1930–1936. Many of these articles were later collected to form books, just as the author had done for his first book, The Religious Problem in Mexico. By the time of the outbreak of the Spanish Civil War in 1936, Sender had published seven novels, five books of journalistic essays, and a book of travel narratives, Madrid-Moscú (Madrid-Moscow), 1934. In addition to writing for La Libertad, for some time (probably between 1930 and 1933) he contributed articles to Solidaridad Obrera (Solidarity of the Workers), a newspaper published by the National Labor Federation (Confederación Nacional de Trabajo) in Barcelona. Sender was an active member of the National Labor Federation, usually known as the CNT, for several years. He never wrote for the newspaper, El Socialista (The Socialist), as once reported.[18]

On January 7, 1934, Sender married Miss Amparo Barayón, a professing Catholic and an amateur pianist, who was born in Zamora and whom Sender had met in Madrid. In 1935 a son, named Ramón, was born to this union; in February of 1936, a daughter, Andrea.

IV *The Civil War, 1936–1939*

On the day the war began, July 18, 1936, Sender was vacationing in his summer cottage at San Rafael in the Guadarrama Mountains. Sending his wife and infant children to his wife's family in Zamora, he immediately made his way alone to Madrid where he offered his services to the Government military forces. Though he had been a persistent and severe critic of many of the policies of the Republican Government, in the hour of that Government's peril he unhesitatingly sided with it against the attacking Rebel forces. In *Counter-Attack in Spain,* 1937, he wrote that resistance to the rebellion was simply "war to the death against the monster. The reaction of Man against the Beast, the assertion of justice against crime."[19] Enlisting as a simple soldier, he soon rose to the rank of major (*comandante*). For a short time he commanded a brigade; later, because of disagreements with Communist elements in command of certain sectors of the Republican front, he was denied command of field troops. He was decorated with the Military Cross of Merit.

In Zamora, in the early days of the war, Sender's wife, Amparo, was arrested by Insurgent forces (when her efforts to arrange an escape to Portugal were discovered, it appears) and placed in jail in that city. On October 11, 1936, she was taken from the jail and executed without a trial. About the same time one of the author's brothers, Manuel, who at that time was the mayor of Huesca in Aragon, was executed, without trial, by Rebel forces.

In 1937, with the aid of the International Red Cross, Sender was able to have his orphaned children taken to Pau in southern France where he arranged for their care during the rest of the war. In the spring of 1938 the Spanish government sent him with José Bergamín, a Spanish writer, Ojier Preteceille, press secretary of the Spanish General Union of Workers, and Carmen Meana, Madrid social worker, on a speaking tour of the United States; their mission was to seek to win support for the Loyalist cause, especially on university campuses. On June 9, 1938, in New York City, Sender addressed a crowd of more than twenty thousand people in Madison Square Garden, fiercely proclaiming even in the face of growing Government defeats in Spain: "The Spanish people will win the war."[20] Soon after his mission to the United States, according to Marcelino Peñuelas, he was assigned the task of founding a war propaganda magazine in Paris, *La Voz de Madrid* (*The Voice of Madrid*); after publication of a few numbers Sender requested to be relieved as director, and returned to Madrid. During the war Sender was a member of Spain's Alliance of Intellectuals for the Defense of Democracy.

Until the novelist himself writes a factual account of his activities during the Civil War (which, as I said before, is not likely to happen), little more than what I have included here can be known for certain about those activities. In *The Five Books of Ariadne* he writes of this period in his life but fact and fantasy are inextricably intertwined. In *The King and the Queen* he has also written about the war, but only in a very oblique way; the war is powerfully present, but only as the realistic background to the inner drama of its protagonist, Rómulo.

In the closing days of 1938 it became obvious that the Republic was doomed. During the general retreat of the Republican forces Sender slipped across the border into France in December of 1938 (and not early in 1939, as usually reported). Perhaps by the time that these words see print he will have returned to his native land, but by mid-1973 he had not returned.

V *France and Mexico, 1939–1942*

Almost nothing is known of Sender's first few weeks in exile. It is probable that he first went to Pau where his infant children were waiting, and that he then took them to Paris. In the French capital, while awaiting passage to Mexico, he, for the benefit of a Spanish refugee organization, directed Zorrilla's famous play, *Don Juan Tenorio*, with a cast of professional and amateur actors at the Théâtre des Ambassadeurs. From references in many of his novels to France and Frenchmen it is evident that his stay in that country left a sharp impression upon him, one not especially flattering to the French. We may take a quota-

tion from *La esfera* (*The Sphere*) as expressive of the resentment he bore the democracies, especially England and France,
for not coming to the aid of the Spanish Republic during the
war. As the train left Paris for the seaport where Saila, the novel's
protagonist and the author's *alter ego,* was to board the ship
that was to take him to America, Sender writes: "He looked with
a certain good humor at the French left on the platform. 'You
poor heroes of conviviality, of forebearance, and condescension.
Fate is going to deal implacably with you.' "[21] It is worth noting
that the action in two of Sender's novels, *La luna de los perros*
(*The Moon of the Dogs*) and *En la vida de Ignacio Morel*
(*In the Life of Ignacio Morel*), occurs in Argenteuil, a Paris
suburb.

Sender left France with his infant children early in March of
1939. His ship landed in New York, and it was here that the
author decided that he should leave his children in the hands of
trusted friends, Mr. and Mrs. Paul West, while he proceeded to
Mexico to establish himself there. Accordingly his son, Ramón,
and his daughter, Andrea, were adopted by the Paul Wests of
New York City. During World War II, while Mr. West was
away from home on military duty, his wife and the Sender
children lived in an old family home in Clarksburg, West Vir-
ginia, but after the war the West family returned to their home
in the New York City area.

Little is known of Sender's activities in Mexico City except
for his prolific literary production. He founded and directed
the publishing firm, Ediciones Quetzal, which published the several books by him during the period 1939–1942. He occasionally
lectured at the National University of Mexico. One of his younger
sisters, Maruja (who figures as a minor character in *Chronicle
of Dawn* with her real name) and her husband also emigrated
to the Mexican capital (where they have remained with their
children). After his entrance into the United States in 1942,
Sender has from time to time visited Mexico.

VI *Since 1942 in the United States*

Having received a Guggenheim Fellowship, Sender emigrated
to the United States in 1942, living first in Santa Fe, New

Mexico. For a while he collaborated on the Inter-American Spanish Research Project at New Mexico Highlands University in Las Vegas.

In 1943 he was elected a corresponding member of the Hispanic Society of America; in 1968 an honorary fellow of the American Association of Teachers of Spanish and Portuguese.

During the academic year of 1943–1944 Sender lectured at the University of Denver, the University of Colorado, and Harvard University. For a short while he lived in Denver; likewise in Boulder and in Estes Park, a resort town thirty-five miles northwest of Boulder. During the academic year of 1944–45 he taught Spanish literature at Amherst College in Massachusetts. During the following two years he had an apartment in New York City, became better acquainted with his two children, and worked as a consultant for the motion picture company, Metro-Goldwyn-Mayer. One of the conditions of employment insisted upon by Sender was that his real name was not to appear on the screen as a collaborator on any movie.

On August 12, 1943, Sender married Florence Hall, who for some time had worked with the Office of Inter-American Affairs of the U.S. Department of State in Washington, D.C. In 1946 he became a naturalized American citizen. In September, 1947, the Aragonese author settled in Albuquerque, New Mexico, buying a home there (630 N. Girard Avenue) and joining the faculty of the University of New Mexico with the rank of Professor of Spanish Literature. Sender continued for sixteen years in his professorial post, until June, 1963. Though he occasionally differed with some of his students, especially with those graduate students who seemed to expect a more traditional or "professorial" or pedantic treatment of Spanish literature in class than Sender gave, he was generally very much liked and admired by his students not only at the University of New Mexico, but also later at the University of Southern California. I was fortunate in being an undergraduate student in two courses taught by him at the University of New Mexico.

Occasionally Don Ramón accepted appointment as a Visiting Professor of Spanish Literature for summer sessions at other institutions; in 1951 he taught at Ohio State University, in 1961 and 1962 at the Inter-American University in Puerto Rico, in

1967 at the University of Washington, and in 1968 at Michigan State University. He was Visiting Professor at the University of California at Los Angeles during the Spring semester of 1962.

During his last academic year at the University of New Mexico, 1962–1963, having been granted a leave-of-absence with pay, Sender traveled to Pau in southern France, where he was reunited with relatives and friends who came from Spain to see him. Except for the fact that he visited France and spent some time in London, little is known of his activities during this visit. Soon after returning to New Mexico he and his wife, Florence Hall Sender, were divorced on September 3, 1963. There had been no children from this union. Shortly afterward, he sold his home in Albuquerque and went to California, where for a time he lived in Hollywood, free from professorial duties. He then bought a home in Manhattan Beach, a noted artists' colony near Los Angeles. It appears, according to Dr. Dorothy McMahon, then Chairman of the Department of Spanish, Italian, and Portuguese of the University of Southern California, that the author missed the human interaction with the students in the classroom, and that he found that his additional free time was not resulting in increased literary productivity. Consequently, it was not surprising that from February, 1965, until June, 1971, Sender was once more in the university classroom, this time in Los Angeles as a Visiting Professor of Spanish Literature at the University of Southern California. When I visited him there in the summer of 1969, he was living in a modest apartment, a short walking distance from the campus. It appears —from the recent upsurge in Senderian titles—that his return to the campus actually resulted in increasing his already prolific production. And this despite an annoying asthmatic condition which has afflicted him since the mid-sixties.

Long ago Sender vowed never to return to Spain except "under morally acceptable conditions." From 1939 until the early 1960's, the sale of his works in Spain was absolutely forbidden. Around 1961 a relaxation in the attitude of the Spanish Government toward Civil War exiles cautiously began; from about 1962 on, the sale of Senderian books in Spain has been permitted. In 1965 Gredos of Madrid published Sender's important book, *Valle-Inclán y la dificultad de la tragedia* (*Valle-Inclán and the Difficulty of Tragedy*), and since that time several new Senderian books and numerous reprints have been published in Spain. Upon publication in Spain of his three-volume auto-biographical novel, *Chronicle of Dawn*, Sender was awarded the Premio de la Literatura (Prize for Literature) of the City of Barcelona for 1966. The literary return of Sender to his native land by 1966 was an established fact; a reprint of *Mr. Witt en el cantón* (*Mr. Witt Among the Rebels*) in 1968, winner in 1935 of the National Prize for Literature, was among the ten best-selling novels in Spain in January, 1969. *Epitalamio del prieto Trinidad* (*Dark Wedding*) was reprinted in 1966 and again in 1969 by the large and distinguished publishing house, Destino, in Barcelona. In 1969 he won the Premio Planeta, Spain's most lucrative literary award (U.S. $15,715), for his novel, *In the Life of Ignacio Morel*. The first edition of *Ignacio* had a press run of fifty-five thousand copies.

Having been invited to give lectures at the Universities of Salamanca and Santander to a conference of writers in Spanish from throughout the world in the summer of 1968, Sender finally decided to return to Spain. He obtained his visa from the Spanish consulate in Los Angeles. At the time a protest against the National Government in the Basque provinces was still in process. At the last minute Government security officers in Madrid became nervous over the anticipated return of Sender, especially when they heard that a group of workers planned to greet the novelist upon his arrival at the Madrid airport. The result was an abrupt cancellation of Sender's visa by the Spanish Government.

It is interesting that Sender, though he has done nothing directly to woo the Spanish worker since the Civil War, is still regarded by many workers as a man on their side, a champion of the underprivileged. He is that but only in a broadly human, never a narrowly partisan way; his attitude is best expressed by him: "What one must do is act as a whole man, not as a fraction of a man. Not to act as men of a social class but as an elemental and generic human being. We do not accept the trickery of class consciousness. Until now such consciousness has given victories only to the enemies of man. . . . Above class interests are those of the human species."[22] It stands repetition that

Sender, despite his early flirtations with the Communists, was never a member of any political party and is not today in any sense a politician. "I believe that I can neither see nor feel politically," he writes in the prologue to *The Five Books of Ariadne.* "I am not capable of lining up with circus dogs barking in rhythm and carrying in their mouth their master's baton. Nor on the other hand do I have the least desire to act as the head of a pack of dogs.... But a writer cannot evade the social circumstances. To maintain oneself insensitive to social problems in our time one must be either a knave or an imbecile."[23] Sender's humanitarian instincts are based on his humanistic view, a profound sense of the essential unity of all mankind, rather than on any sociopolitical credo or philosophy.

CHAPTER 2

Aragon, Spain, and Beyond

I Aragon

S ENDER, like any other author, is a product of his own
country and historical period. In this chapter I briefly consider the forces and influences which have molded him as a
man and as an author, taking up first his heritage as an Aragonese, then as a Spaniard, and lastly as a man deeply aware of the
international ideological and artistic movements of his time. I
view the formative elements in Sender's life as three concentric
circles with Aragon occupying the center, then Spain, and the
world itself as the outer circle. At one and the same time Don
Ramón is very Aragonese, very Spanish, and very much a citizen of the world.

It is said that every Spaniard has two countries: his *patria
chica* (little country) and his *patria grande* (big country). The
term "The Spains" is still descriptive of Spain. Sender's *patria
chica* is Aragon. Because of the novelist's longstanding roots in
rural Upper Aragon, it is not surprising that he has never ceased
to consider himself deeply Aragonese and a rural dweller (*campesino*). He states so clearly in the important prologue to his
novel, *Los cinco libros de Ariadna* (*The Five Books of Ariadne*):
"Like every Spaniard, I have had my adventures. The risks have
been many, but so far the repertory of the simplest and most
basic values of the people of my land has helped me. Not of
the Spaniard of the city . . . but perhaps of the tribes from Upper
Aragon north of the Ebro. I do not say this romantically . . . but
simply with a modest desire for accuracy."[1]

The Aragonese are noted for their proud and individualistic
spirit. Salvador de Madariaga, the great Spanish scholar, wrote:
"The Aragonese is the most primitive, perhaps the most genuine,
representative of the distinctly Spanish features. Spontaneous,

frank, he is apt to form extreme opinions; he is uncompromising, stubborn, richer in intuition than in conscious intellect, independent, proud and individualistic. Goya was an Aragonese."[2] One might add that Joaquín Costa, noted for his fiercely independent spirit, as well as Baltasar Gracián, author of *El Criticón* (*The Hyper-Critic*) in the seventeenth century, were also Aragonese.

Historically Aragon has been a leader in achieving a high degree of autonomy for the various regions in Spain. In the Middle Ages the Aragonese were responsible, according to George Northup, for two "great charters of liberty ... outstanding documents in the history of European jurisprudence,"[3] the General Privilege, 1283, and the Privilege of Union, 1287. Through the marriage of Queen Isabel of Castile and King Ferdinand of Aragon and the union of their respective kingdoms into a political federation in 1479, the first step toward Spanish national unity was taken. National unity in Spain, however, has always been rather tenuous, given the strong tendency toward individualism and regionalism of Spanish subjects. In a book published and distributed by the Spanish Information Service in 1971, we read: "The Spanish concept of the dignity of the person is intimately related to the vigour of local and regional sentiments, that continue standing five hundred years after the consummation of the unity of Aragon and Castile."[4] Sender attests to the "vigour of local and regional sentiments" by asserting in 1957: "For me the nation does not exist, but the territory and mine is Aragon, and I stick to it."[5]

It is not surprising that the author is not only proud of his Aragonese heritage and background, but that he exhibits in his character and in his work the fierce independence, sense of human dignity, the individualism, and obstinacy which so characterize the Aragonese as a people. Three of his very finest novels depict life in his native region: *A Man's Place, Chronicle of Dawn*, and *Requiem for a Spanish Peasant*. His long historical novel, *Byzantium*, is a tribute to the fighting spirit and superhuman endurance of Aragonese soldiers. Long before him, however, Benito Pérez Galdós had portrayed in his novel, *Zaragoza*, the heroism and glorious obstinacy of the Aragonese in their epic defense of Saragossa against the French in 1808 and 1809.

II *Spain*

A. Literature

The vast and rich literature of Spain was Sender's to explore.
Wherein does Hispanic literature differ from the literature of
other Western European countries? Salvador de Madariaga
wrote: "While France and Italy are eminently intellectual and
critical, Spain is eminently intuitive and creative."[6] Spain, we
are reminded, produced such mystics as St. Theresa, St. John of
the Cross, and Fray Luis de León. In general, Spanish writers
have been noted for their intuition and brilliant imaginativeness
rather than for systematic and sustained development of literary
movements or schools.

In each national literary tradition certain themes tend to be
emphasized and repeated. Though such themes may not be
exclusive to that tradition, they are sometimes singularly expressed and given special vigor in the literature of that nation.
In Spanish letters, leading themes, recurring through the centuries, include the following: the search for the Absolute, death,
curiosity about the world beyond death, hunger and struggle
(exemplified by the picaresque novel), life—dream or reality,
the impossible dream or ideal (e.g., Don Quixote's creation of
Dulcinea), and the Don Juan myth or theme. These and other
themes so characteristic of Hispanic literature abound in Senderian works.

Spanish literature is perhaps the most "human" of literatures.
Though man is ultimately the primary concern of all literatures,
the various literatures of the world reflect their concern for
man in different manners and with different emphases. In Spanish literature, for example, man tends to be stripped of adjectives;
insofar as possible only the individual *man*—Unamuno's man of
"flesh and bones"—remains. Spain's man tends to be neither all
body nor all soul, but an indestructible fusion of both elements—
the whole man. In philosophical terms this attitude is called
"Integralism." Martin Lebowitz comments: "But what is a well-
balanced philosophy? . . . it seems clear that philosophy is well
balanced when it succeeds in accommodating both the ideal
and the real, the desirable and the actual—in other words, feeling and thought. That [this] is no easy task the record shows."[7]

The Spaniard always has at least a little of Don Quixote in him. Objective rationalism has never flourished in Spain. The Spaniard insists on keeping both his heart and his head, both irrational sentiment and logic. And is he not right? In recent years even the most avid rationalists admit the impossibility of total elimination of subjective elements from scientific research. Human thinking may be dominantly "objective" or "subjective," but it can never be entirely one or the other.

Closely identified with Spanish Integralism, if indeed not part and parcel with it, is the Spanish humanistic tradition which has made Hispanic literature one of the world's most democratic. Democracy, as I use the term here, primarily means profound respect for the intrinsic and unique worth of every person. Paradoxically, however, at the political level democracy seems always to fail or to function only falteringly in Spain. Yet, despite Spanish political history, the dignity of the Spanish is well known. Although there are class divisions in Spain, snobbishness among Spaniards is rare. Servant and master engage naturally in conversation. It is true, as Madariaga says, "He [the Spaniard] is neither a citizen of an equalitarian state, nor a partner in a national society, nor a subject in an empire. He is a man."[8] There is an old Spanish saying: "Man's first profession is to be a man." This natural humanism which pervades Spanish life and literature has its origins in Greek and Roman thought as well as in the Christian concept of the spiritual dignity and equality of all men in God's sight. The Renaissance was characterized intellectually by an increased interest in man as man. Comments Sender: "Spiritually, the world still lives in our day off the heritage of the Renaissance; and Cervantes represents the Spanish Renaissance in all its plenitude, namely, the triumph of the free spirit, which is capable of interpreting man and the human and of discovering in him what might be academically styled 'the constants of universality.'"[9]

Spanish literature, even when anticlerical, may well be called Catholic. In a cultural sense Sender is "Catholic," though he rejects the Church as an institution. Education in Spain was, and is, almost completely dominated by the Church. The Inquisition was not formally abolished there until 1931.

Sender has drunk deeply from the well of his national literary heritage. He bears notable resemblance to four Spanish authors whom he once said had greatly influenced him: Fernando de Rojas, Francisco Quevedo, Pío Baroja, and Ramón del Valle-Inclán.[10] Sender's strange fusion of the harshest of realism with flights of lyrical fantasy recall the two levels of realism and fantasy in *La Celestina* (*The Procuress*) by Rojas at the end of the fifteenth century as well as some of Valle-Inclán's later works. His bitter satire, tendency to caricature, and grim humor bring to mind Quevedo, the seventeenth-century author of *El buscón* (*The Cheat*) and *Los sueños* (*The Visions*). Sender's preoccupation with social, moral, and metaphysical problems as well as his direct, unaffected, verbal style may owe more than we know to Baroja, the leading figure of the twentieth-century Spanish novel. Like Baroja, Sender is a writer of substance, always with something worthwhile to say, and with little, if any, respect for mere form or style. Though Sender insists that it was Valle-Inclán the man, more than the literary artist, who influenced him, one can point to passages in Sender's works which in their juxtaposition of the grotesque and bizarre with the lyrically innocent in search of poetic effects are clearly reminiscent of the great Galician writer. I may also point out as more than coincidence the frequent treatment in Sender's works of superstition and of witchcraft, themes which also fascinated Valle-Inclán.

B. Politics

"Representative novelists of modern Spain scorn the menial task of jester or talemonger; they profess to play the role of interpreters of their complex social scene and its problems," writes John Reid.[11] Despite Modernism, "art for art's sake" or the theory of "pure" literature has had little acceptance by Spanish writers. Since no author lives in a social vacuum—and perhaps least of all the Hispanic author—Sender has a definite conception of the sociopolitical world, and he clearly expresses that viewpoint in his work. Yet his deeply human interest has saved him from becoming a mere writer of social protest novels.

The need for agragrian reform in Spain has long been a live issue among Spanish intellectuals. During the years of the

Spanish Republic in the thirties, it was an especially passionate issue, perhaps the central problem of Spain. The need for land reform is an important theme in Sender's novels: *Trip to the Village of Crime, A Man's Place,* and *Requiem for a Spanish Peasant.* The post-Civil War regime daily lives with the problems engendered by what might be termed "feudal" landholding practices in Spain. Even the Spanish Information Service, the mouthpiece for the Spanish Government to the world outside Spain, admitted in a book published in 1971 that general economic progress in some areas of the country had been set back by "some static social forms and an inequitable distribution of property."[12] The same book reports an emigration of 100,840 Spaniards to European countries (principally to France, Germany, Switzerland, and England) in 1969, which is approximately the average annual figure for the preceding ten years. Many, if not most, of these emigrating Spaniards are landless peasants. About eighty percent of them return to Spain after two or three years, according to the same source.

If it is true, as Charles Neider says, that "the nineteenth century was Hellenistic, with emphasis on the individual and the sensuous and the twentieth is Hebraic, with emphasis on the moral and the political,"[13] then Sender's consuming interest in moral and sociopolitical issues reveals him to be a twentieth-century man. Sender and a few other Spanish writers of his generation sought through their writing to awaken a social consciousness among their fellow compatriots; some, including Sender, also actively participated in politics and revolutionary activities. It was largely through their efforts that the dictatorship of Primo de Rivera, as well as the monarchy of Alphonso XIII, was liquidated in 1931, and the Second Spanish Republic established. Among writers, however, they were in the minority since a kind of rather sterile aestheticism was in vogue among most Spanish authors of Sender's age during the twenties and thirties.

III   *Beyond the Pyrenees*

Deeply involved in Spanish life and almost thirty-eight years old when he fled Spain, Sender's essential character and his direction in life had already been solidified. From early youth he apparently had been wide open to the main intellectual and artistic currents of his time from beyond the Pyrenees. He learned to read French at an early age. His travel abroad—to the Soviet Union and to the United States—was mentioned in Chapter 1. Though forty-one when he settled in the United States, he learned to speak English sufficiently well to be able to answer questions directed to him as the invited guest on a radio program in Los Angeles in 1966; his reading ability in English, incidentally, is even superior to his speaking ability.

It is obvious to anyone reading him that Sender has assimilated the most advanced thinking of the twentieth century. It is doubtful, in fact, whether any Spanish writer of this century can match him in his penetrating understanding of the world outside Spain. The novel, as do the theater and other genres, reflects the changing thought-forms of the last half century, especially in the Western world. From his first novel in 1930 until the present, Sender's novels constitute a veritable testimony of the main crises of our time and of their effects upon man and man's view of himself.

Among the foreign political "isms" finding a fertile breeding ground in Spain during the twenties and the early thirties, Anarchism, Socialism, and Communism were powerful forces among the masses as well as among liberal intellectuals. Anarchism was scarcely "foreign" to Spain; indeed, *as an attitude*, it seems always to have been a strong force in that country. The passion of the Iberian Anarchists for liberty and their abhorrence for any kind of coercion or centralization of authority together with the traditional Spanish tendency toward separatism (and dictatorship, I might add) weakened the Second Spanish Republic, and contributed, perhaps decisively, to its eventual defeat by organized military force in 1939. It will not be necessary to discuss here the distinctions between Socialism and Communism; in Spain, then as now, the practical differences between these two political theories were largely in the degree of radicalism, Socialism being the more moderate in its goals and less revolutionary in its methodology. It must be remembered that the Soviet experiment was still fresh, and many leading European intellectuals still cherished a rather naive faith in the efficacy of political solutions to socioeconomic problems and believed fervently in the real possibility of the establishment of a kind of Communistic or Socialistic Utopia.[14] Neither the Socialists nor the Communists, however, were able to cooperate with one another in Spain; in the end the Civil War came and the three foreign "isms"—Socialism, Communism, and Anarchism—along with the Second Spanish Republic were devastatingly crushed. In the process a million Spaniards died. Sender's flirtation with both the Anarchists and the Communists in his early years is well known. As a youth he was once a member of a group of seven Anarchists;[15] his Communistic leanings are evident in much of his work discussed in later chapters (although he never joined the Party). It appears that he was never involved with the Socialists.

Many of Spain's leading intellectual and literary figures either died in the Civil War or exiled themselves (to avoid almost certain death had they remained in Spain) at the conclusion of the conflict. For writers such as Francisco Ayala, Arturo Barea and Ramón Sender, the defeat of the Republic was a traumatic experience; though they may have been disillusioned as to the effectiveness of bringing about desired social changes through political means alone, they never lost their firm faith in the essential justice of the Republican cause nor in man himself, nor in man's need to continue to dream his Utopian dreams. Sender's personal struggle with himself to overcome bleak despair at the end of the Spanish War and to maintain hope forms the substance of his book, *The Sphere.*

A few months after the collapse of the Spanish Republic early in 1939, Hitler's troops moved into France. A state of demoralization pervaded France and Spain. Man not only began to despair of ever improving the social and political circumstances of his life, but seemed to lose faith in himself as a man, in his cosmic fate. A year earlier Jean-Paul Sartre had published *Nausée (Nausea)*; in 1942 *L'Etranger (The Stranger)* by Albert Camus appeared. Modern Existentialism, a philosophy of despair which regarded life as essentially absurd, meaningless, spread among the intellectuals of Europe and eventually to the rest of the world. Spain's reading public had, long before Sartre, been exposed to the Existentialist works of Miguel de Unamuno, and José Ortega y Gasset. In time Existentialism has come to be reflected in almost all of the leading literature of our time; it has filtered down to affect the thinking and life styles of university students the world over, especially in the Western world.

Essentially, modern Existentialism represents a rejection of the points of view which had dominated Western man's thinking in the nineteenth century and, to choose an arbitrary date, more or less in the twentieth century up until 1939. World War II shook man's faith in all abstract systems—philosophical, theological, political. The major systems which Existentialism repudiated taught the evolution or projection of man toward some ideal future. The promises of Catholicism, Communism, Humanism, even Darwinianism, were rejected in favor of the *present existence* of the individual—the *here* and *now*. *Processes* were rejected in favor of the *concrete situation*. No more talk of the *origin* and the *goal* or *destiny* of man, either as an individual or as a collectivity. Only the present matters, the fleeting moment that cuts between past and future. The only "process" is man living, conceived of as his projecting himself, faring forth, in time and space. Darwinian evolution, for example, which seeks to explain the origin and subsequent development of man is rejected along, of course, with all religious systems as well as Hegelian Dialecticalism. The Existentialist "process" is seen as a movement of only one dimension, flat, and not as a vertical progression toward a destiny or goal.

Spanish writers tend to adjust foreign philosophies, attitudes, movements, and ideas to their own unique Spanish circumstances, way of life, and world view. The result is that such influences are usually manifested in Spain in a very diluted form, or altered so as hardly to be recognized. The so-called *tremendismo* of Camilo José Cela's first novel, *The Family of Pascual Duarte*, in 1942, and of Carmen Laforet's first novel, *Nada* (*Nothing*) in 1944, reflects vaguely the Existentialist posture. Both works are basically nihilistic in viewpoint and create a sombre, apathetic, and desperate atmosphere, with interest centered around the individual protagonists. They mark the revival of the Spanish novel after the Civil War, and 1942 has come to be regarded as the date of the beginning of the contemporary Spanish novel.

Since the Spanish War the most vigorous literary genre in

Spain has been the novel. In the Spanish novel—and I mean the novel written by Spaniards both in and out of Spain—the influence of Existentialism may be seen in the renewed interest in the individual and concrete man, ordinary and unheroic man, often vaguely referred to as the antihero. Clear examples of new emphasis upon the individual and his personal existence are Cela's *The Family of Pascual Duarte* and Laforet's *Nothing*. The protagonist of each of these novels is a lone and alienated person, living without a definite goal and with no firm morality. During the following three decades their basic personality profiles were to appear again and again in the narratives of Ana María Matute, Francisco Ayala, Antonio Zunzunegui, Juan Goytisolo, Jesús Fernández Santos, and others. *El Jarama* (*The Jarama*), 1956, the celebrated novel by Rafael Sánchez Ferlosio, has no protagonist but succeeds in communicating the alienation, the purposelessness, apathy, and desperation of its many characters. The interest is upon the individual, no matter how trivial his life appears to be, and his relations with "the other" (people, things, abstractions).

The Spanish War and its aftermath of general loss of faith in traditional values intensified Sender's interest in the meaning of personal existence. His first two postwar novels, *Proverb of Death* and *A Man's Place*, are cases in point. Saila, the protagonist of *Proverb* (later expanded and retitled *The Sphere*) resembles an Existentialist hero in his aloneness, in his rejection of all existing abstract thought-systems (rationalism, Marxism, Catholicism, bourgeois morality, etc.), his emphasis upon the present, and in his quiet but desperate search for meaning for himself. Yet Saila is not an Existentialist, at least not in the Sartrian sense. He has, in a sense, gone "beyond Existentialism" to become a mystic, albeit a very twentieth-century and unconventional one, who though recognizing his existential "loneness" yet seeks comfort in his personal, abstract, philosophical-theological theory of the sphere.[16] In *A Man's Place* the protagonist, Sabino, a man so ignored by society that he is not its most insignificant person but a "nonperson" in his Spanish community, becomes first a symbol of the Spanish (*pueblo*), then of individual man today. When Sabino is absent from his "place" in society (as he was for fifteen years), grave repercussions occur, repercussions which must be interpreted as the protest of some fatality, blind or otherwise. Except for its supreme focus upon the individual in which, incidentally, it coincides with Existentialism, *A Man's Place* is not Existentialist, at least not in the *modern* sense of this word.[17]

A phenomenon which seems to be related to the Existentialist mood of the last three decades is the tendency for plots to disappear and to be replaced with situations. Thus we have novels of situation (a parallel development has occurred in the theater). The protagonist as conventionally conceived also has tended to disappear, often to be replaced by a group of people. Notable examples in Spain are *The Hive* by Cela, *The Jarama* by Ferlosio, and *La noria* (*The Water Wheel*) by Luis Romero. The suppression of the protagonist is in line with Existentialist thinking that no individual is more important than another; each is of supreme importance to himself. In his earliest novels Sender seems to have anticipated the new trends of the mid-century; of his pre-Civil War novels only one, *Mr. Witt Among the Rebels*, has a plot and a very tenuous one at that; his first novel, *Pro Patria*, simply tells of the experiences of a Spanish soldier in the African campaign; *Public Order*, 1931, describes the author's sensations, thoughts, and experiences while in prison, and is quite clearly a novel of situation; *El Verbo se higo sexo* (*The Word Became Sex*), 1931, is a novelized version of the life of St. Theresa; *Seven Red Sundays*, 1932, simply narrates (with much commentary intermixed) the seven days of an abortive revolt in Madrid; *Viaje a la aldea del crimen* (*Trip to the Village of Crime*), 1934, is a straightforward account of an insurrection by Andalusian peasants and its brutal repression by Government Assault Troops; and *La noche de las cien cabezas* (*The Night of One Hundred Heads*), 1934, is little more than a running satirical commentary by the author on a hundred heads which fall into a Madrid cemetery during a windstorm one night; they represent a cross section of corrupt Spanish society.

Indeed, only a few of Sender's "novels" have what one might call a plot in the conventional sense of the term; they are *Mr. Witt Among the Rebels, A Man's Place, Dark Wedding, The King and the Queen, Requiem for a Spanish Peasant* and *In the*

Life of Ignacio Morel. Even in these narratives the situation is more vivid than the actual plot development.

A discussion of the contemporary novel in any Western country must give some attention to Sigmund Freud and Karl Jung. Their discovery of the unconscious has deeply and permanently changed European literature of this century, although in Spanish literature the effects may not be so visible as in other Western literatures. Yet, though perhaps more subtle and somewhat later than in other countries, the influence of the discovery of the unconscious has been incalculable there also. The highly acclaimed *El tiempo del silencio* (*The Time of Silence*) by Luis Martín-Santos in 1961, for example, is a novel which clearly derived from Joyce's *Ulysses*. Francisco Ayala, Max Aub, and Sender clearly are deeply influenced by modern psychology. The hallucinatory atmosphere, dreamlike scenes, dreams and dreams within dreams, the use of interior monologue to express the "stream of consciousness," surrealistic touches, and the contrasting of the world of the unconscious with the conscious world of appearances in Sender's works attest to the influence, direct or indirect, of Freud and Jung.

In Sender the strong mystical vein in Spanish literature, especially of the Golden Age, and modern psychology converge. For him the unconscious becomes the "abyss," the source of poetic inspiration, heroism, and holiness. Sender is a literary mystic who highly resembles the French Surrealists in his conception of the process of literary creation. For him literary creation consists primarily not in commentary or reflection upon what is already known (the task of the academics), but in the discovery of new material in the twilight zone of "transcendental consciousness" where consciousness and the unconscious supposedly intersect. The new material is assumed to be conjured up, as it were, from the unconscious, that realm of "mysteries and miracles." André Breton called the exploration of the unconscious "the great modern tradition" originating from Baudelaire's:

Plonger au fond du gouffre, Enfer ou Ciel qu'importe!
Au fond de l'Inconnu pour trouver du nouveau!

(To plunge to the bottom of the abyss, Hell or Heaven
    what matters it!
To the bottom of the Unknown, to find something new!)

The mere discovery, of course, of some truth or beauty in
the "unconscious" is not enough to produce a work of art. To
communicate beauty or poetic truth there is no substitute for
the artist's talent and reason. My purpose here, however, is not
to justify the classification of Sender as a Surrealist (after the
manner of the French Surrealists), but merely to indicate that
at least some of his works exhibit a degree of affinity with
French Surrealism. The subject needs further study with clear
distinctions made between surrealism in the general sense, the
kind of stepping beyond the bounds of ordinary reality one
finds so often in the best of Spanish writers through the centuries (Cervantes, Calderón, Quevedo, Valle-Inclán, for example) and the tenets of the French Surrealists especially as expressed in their Manifestoes of 1924 and 1930.[18] It may well be,
as Julia Uceda has said, that Surrealism "serves him [Sender] in
advancing more in search of a reality of essences which he
frequently expresses by poetic means."[19] In other words, Sender
has availed himself of the liberating influence of French Surrealism in his search to express what he calls "essential reality," a
reality of essences, the "universal," which is neither an individual
reality nor a "photographic" reality of appearances. It must be
remembered that Sender ever seeks to achieve levels of poetic
reality in his novels; apparent reality in his works generally,
but not always, serves as the point of departure or the springboard for the attempt to express a deeper or higher reality, an
"essential reality" which can infuse an entire work with a
lyrical light.

Sender, writes Marcelino Peñuelas, "is interested only mar-
ginally in external or physical reality."[20] His novels are in this
sense in line with the *antirealistic* direction of fiction during
recent decades. Since ordinary reality in the manner of a Balzac,
a Dickens, or a Pérez Galdós in the late nineteenth century
can best be done today by the cinema, the novelist must portray a deeper and inner reality. Both Miguel de Unamuno and
Pío Baroja saw the need for the "inner realism" at the turn of

the century. Valle-Inclán was noted (and criticized) for his rejection of a too-narrowly-conceived realism. Franz Kafka of Czechoslovakia is a modern example of a writer who has scorned outer realism in favor of a purely subjective world of "reality"; Sender, however, has by no means forsaken so-called objective reality to the same extent as have Kafka and some of the Surrealists; his novels are firmly rooted in a believable, external reality which often serves as a kind of springboard to the realm of the super-real or fantastic.

One writes best about what he knows best, Sender believes. It has already been seen that Sender's novels are highly autobiographic. The most explicitly autobiographical of his novels is his nine-part, three-volume series, *Chronicle of Dawn*. In his autobiographical tendency Sender helps form a trend among twentieth-century European writers, including Spanish. Unamuno, Azorín, and Baroja of the Generation of 1898, all wrote autobiographical books based on their childhood memories and frequently inserted into their other works autobiographical elements.

More recent autobiographical novels, both Spanish and European, however, are written with a new purpose in mind; they are written "as a process of discovery," say Edith Helman and Doris K. Arjona.[21] According to them, novelists of today "seem to feel the need to return to their origins, to earliest childhood, like Freud in his investigations, in order to try to discover how they went astray, how they came to be estranged from their own world. . . . They evoke past experiences in interior monologs as a means of better explaining the present."[22] Once again we may infer the influence of Freud, direct or indirect. Sender wrote *Chronicle of Dawn* to explore the sources of the idealistic faith which led him and many others to risk their lives in defense of the Second Spanish Republic; his is no escapist return to childhood, but rather one of purposeful research.

When asked to name his favorite authors from world literature, Sender replied: "Rojas, Cervantes, Quevedo, in Spain. Bacon, in England; Montaigne, in France. I mean, among the classics. They are the teachers of all of us. Then, the Russians and Stendhal. As they also are to everybody. Among the moderns I like William Faulkner, Edmund Wilson and Ralph Ellison in the

United States, and Celine in France. In England, D. H. Lawrence and some of the young writers."[23] In a taped interview at the University of Southern California on June 7, 1966, Sender stated that Simone Weil, the French mystic and scholar (1909–1942), whose work was not published until after her death, had been the greatest single influence upon him during the previous two decades. He no doubt was referring to her as a thinker and seeker after God more than as a writer *per se,* an influence heightened by the memory of his short acquaintance with her in Barcelona during the Civil War.

I can only begin here to indicate Sender's sensitivity to literary and intellectual currents outside of Spain; a developed treatment would mean the writing of another book. I have suggested only a few of the varied influences and forces of contemporary times which have shaped Sender the man and the novelist. The twentieth century has been a tumultuous period, bewilderingly rich in ideological and artistic currents. And, more important, it has been marked by a series of catastrophes to disillusion man. Sender is a man who has looked the evil of this hour fully in the face, while yet maintaining his primitive faith in the ultimate dignity of the individual human being. Indeed, as an author he has accepted the stupendous task of seeking to define the nature of evil.

CHAPTER 3

Pre-Exile Novels, 1930-1938

I Imán (Pro Patria), 1930

IMÁN, whose English translation is "magnet," is important not only as Sender's first novel, but also because in style and human content it accurately foreshadows the prolific Senderian novelistic production of the next four decades. Even today it remains as one of Sender's very finest novels. Though sales volume is not necessarily a criterion of literary excellence, it has probably sold more copies than any of his other novels; as stated in Chapter 1, it was soon translated into ten foreign languages, and partially into an eleventh. It was more successful outside of Spain than in Spain although a second Spanish edition, an inexpensive one, of thirty thousand copies was published in 1933. Its English translation, by James Cleugh, was published in London under the title *Earmarked for Hell*, in 1934, and the following year in Boston under a different title, *Pro Patria*. I shall henceforth refer to it by its American title, *Pro Patria*, and all quotations from the novel will be from this edition; page references are in parentheses.

Recently, three Senderian critics have praised *Pro Patria* most highly. Francisco Carrasquer, who devotes fifty-one pages of his book, *"Imán" y la novela histórica de Sender* (*"Imán" and Sender's Historical Novels*), to a discussion of the work calls it "a great novel." "So great," he adds, "that one cannot understand how a first work like it did not definitively consecrate its author."[1] "For its contribution of simplicity, for the virile value and the lesson of frankness that *Pro Patria* meant in its day, this work would have to pass—for as much reason as Cela's *Pascual Duarte* passed in other circumstances—as a renovating and vivifying milestone in the history of contemporary Spanish literature," Carrasquer concludes.[2] Marcelino C. Peñuelas in a conversation once told Sender: "It is a great novel, without doubt. One of your best novels. You have a few novels the equal of *Imán,* but none better."[3] Rafael Bosch praises the poetic effects achieved by the book's imagery.[4] Only recently have critics begun to discover that most, if not all,-of the major elements found in Sender's vast novelistic production are present in his first novel, hitherto generally and mistakenly regarded simply as a realistic account of the Moroccan campaign, another anti-war book in the style of the best seller in 1929, Erich Maria Remarque's *Im Westen nichts Neues* (*All Quiet on the Western Front*).

In 1921 the Moorish chieftain Abd el Krim, in a protest against Spanish colonial policy in Morocco, led his Riff tribesmen in a bloody revolt against Spanish troops garrisoned in Spanish Morocco. His forces captured Annual, a Spanish stronghold, and its outposts, in a campaign costing twelve thousand Spanish lives. In *Pro Patria,* Viance, a Spanish private, and Antonio, a Spanish sergeant who had been, like Sender, a journalist in civilian life (and who bears one of Sender's names: Ramón José Antonio y Blas), alternate with an "omniscient" author in telling the story of Viance's participation in that disaster. Viance and Antonio were both assigned to the defense of an outpost of Annual called "R." in the novel just before both Annual and R. were overrun by the Moroccan troops.

The outbreak in 1921 had been preceded by a long series of earlier clashes and irritations between the Spaniards and the Moors. In 1909 Riff tribesmen, through their fierce attacks, forced temporary suspension of the Spanish Government's attempt to build a railway from the seacoast base of Melilla into the back country, where Spanish concessionaires had mining interests. Over the sometimes violent protest in Catalonia especially, but also in other regions of Spain, the central Government persisted in its colonial policies, calling out reserves to put down Riff opposition. Thus Abd el Krim's uprising in 1921 was merely another episode in Spain's festering Moroccan problem. Sender in 1923 was one of thousands of young Spaniards who were conscripted into the army and sent to Africa.

Since Sender did not arrive in Morocco as a soldier until at least two years after the defeat at Annual, he personally could not have experienced the events related in the novel. Despite his lack of firsthand participation in the gruesome events related in the book, Sender has admirably succeeded in reconstructing the horrors, the brutalities, the injustices, and the utter stupidity of the war.

The narrative falls into three major divisions: I, The Camp—The Relief; II, Annual—The Catastrophe; and III, Escape—War—Discharge—The Peace of the Dead. Part I, consisting of 101 pages in the English translation, sets the tone and atmosphere for the rest of the novel; from the outset a vivid picture of the filth, rigors, privations, injustices and boredom of life in camp R., an outpost of Annual, is painted. There is an implied protest against the uselessness and senselessness of the campaign. Though the book begins with Antonio (Sender), a sergeant present at R., narrating in the first person, it soon introduces Viance, the Spanish private who then starts telling his own story. Later an omniscient author intervenes; most of the rest of the story is told by him in the third person, although there are occasional brief returns to first-person narrative by both Viance and Antonio. But the novel is always Viance's story. Some critics have criticized this shifting of narrative points of view, calling it confusing.[5] In this respect it seems to have anticipated the trend during the last decade to write novels with changing points of view and perspective.

The defenders of R. watch as a Spanish force of three hundred men whom they have just relieved leave the camp to make their way to Annual, visible a few miles away. As the sun sets over the desert, they see the three hundred men destroyed by Moorish troops who seem to spring out of nowhere. The Moors then intensify their attack upon R. and finally overrun it in a horrendous and bloody scene during which Viance somehow or other is able to escape alone. Part I ends with the capture and destruction of R.

The second part, consisting of 142 pages in a book totalling 295, provides the main narrative thrust of the novel. It relates Viance's nightmare odyssey across sixty miles of Moor-infested desert in search of territory still held by the Spaniards. First approaching Annual, he learns that it also has fallen. For days he deliriously drags himself across the desert, discovering that one camp after another (Dar Drius, Tistutin, Nador) at which he had expected to find safety had been captured by the enemy; the wanderer's pace is agonizing; repeatedly Viance, sick from his wounds, more dead than alive from hunger, thirst, and exhaustion, reaches the utter limits of human endurance; he survives only because of the blind force of living things to continue living though death would have been a relief. Part II ends with his capture by Moorish troops in the very outskirts of Melilla (still in the hands of the Spaniards) seven days after his escape from R.

The third part begins with Viance's escape from the Moors on the very day of his surrender to them, his safe arrival in Melilla, the grotesquely inhuman treatment of him by Spanish officialdom there which refuses him admittance to the hospital, leaving him to sleep on the street like a dog and sending him immediately back into battle. For having hurled a bottle in rage against the doctor who pronounced him fit for duty, Viance later was sentenced to two extra years of service. The two years are passed over in silence, and in a kind of epilogue we see Viance, a sad, demoralized, beaten shell of a man (he felt that his real self had died in Africa), freshly discharged and returning after a five-year absence to visit his native Aragonese village, only to find that it now lies under the surface of a new dam created in his absence. This discovery accentuates his despair. "Formerly, even at the worst periods of the campaign, he possessed a solid moral foundation for his personality. It was composed of his childhood, his village, the familiar fields, the streets. . . . His life had begun to invade infinity and had no basis, nowhere to set one's feet to take off into space" (294). He contemplates suicide as he learns that there is no work for him, that the inhabitants of the new village constructed to replace the one submerged by the dam show him neither consideration nor respect for his military service. In bitter irony, the novel ends as a cheap female cafe dancer, seeing Viance, repeats " 'Viva! for Spain!' three times, in weird, gypsy harmonies, waggling her hips" (295).

Viance is both an individual soldier and a symbol of the Spanish underprivileged masses, the *pueblo*. Though his inner resentment against the injustices and abuses to his dignity as a

human being that he had suffered in the army made him assume
an outward appearance of indifference, and even stupidity, he
was, all things considered, a truly admirable human being,
sound in body and mind. There is a parallel between the treatment meted out to Viance by his officers and the treatment of
the Spanish lower classes by the upper classes through the
centuries. It is in this implied parallel between Viance and the
Spanish people that the element of social protest in the book
is most clearly seen. *Pro Patria* is not a pacifist book; its protest
is not so much against war in general as it is against the Spanish
Moroccan War in particular and its general mismanagement by
the Spanish Government. Viance does not really believe in the
justice of the Spanish cause; to him the rout of the Spanish
forces might well be the vengeance of some kind of Divine
Justice. "The right of the stronger is fixed by some cosmic power,
and logic and legality are his alone" (187). Yet the author never
forgets that the individual, though he be the weakest member
of a society, has a personal responsibility for the actions of
that society.

Viance was to blame, just as Rivero and Otazu and Piqueras
were.

They were all culpable, because one man's as good as another, and
if one man says yes another can say no. Well, what then? The fact
of the matter was that they had all said yes without knowing what
they were saying, and now they went about asking for bullets through
their heads because their heads hadn't had the sense, when they
were put to it, to make a reasonable reply. (221)

The book's social protest is implicit from the events and action
of the novel itself, and not superimposed artificially by the
comments of the author except for an occasional lapse, inten-
tional or otherwise.

Sender's novelistic art has no doubt matured and improved
through the decades, yet one sees in *Pro Patria* the sure hand
of Sender the novelist: a direct, sober, verbal style, an impersonal
distancing of the author from the work, the same grim—sometimes gruesome—humor present even in his latest novels, the
same interweaving of objective and subjective realities to create

the novel's own private world, the harshest of realistic detail alongside lyrical and metaphysical fantasy, the flight into delirium and dreams which sometimes cast a surrealistic spell over the action, and the everpresent probing of ultimate reality, mystery. Sender does not write with what one may call elegance, and for that reason his novels at the hand of expert translators have generally suffered little in translation.

On sentinel duty facing an imminent attack and having witnessed the extermination of three hundred Spanish troops just as darkness fell

[Viance] succumbed to terrifying but vague reflections. The plain, if it had been visible, would be a dreadful sight. No doubt the Moorish cavalry was already pursuing the fugitives, hunting them down with scimitar and lance. Those who escaped could only reach the wire at Annual by a miracle. And all that, happening under the indifference of the starry sky, so far away, to men who had been forgotten even by those they loved, suggested that some vast mistake had been made, some vast responsibility incurred. But where? And who was guilty? The night deepened. "Nice sort of hours these are. One never goes off duty."

Shots rang out in the distance at intervals, followed by cries in Arabic. (98–99)

The fusion of external reality with Viance's inner, subjective world in the above passage is typical of the entire novel, as well as the haunting question of human guilt.

There are many scenes of unflinching realism comparable to the one quoted below which describes a wounded soldier. Such scenes could be regarded as *tremendista* (tremendous), though that term was not applied to Spanish letters until 1942 when Camilo José Cela published his first novel, *The Family of Pascual Duarte*.

His trousers were stained red, as though he were urinating blood. He retired a little, loosened his belt, and squatted on his hams. The blood from his intestines poured in a thick, red stream. Then he rose, yellower still in the face, and pushing down his trousers exposed his naked stomach and made an inspection of the wound. He seemed a grotesque symbol, to Viance, of the whole tragedy, standing there with his sexual organs uncovered beneath his mangled stomach. (230–31)

The Spaniards are reduced to drinking urine, and in his extremity of hunger Viance is saved from eating human flesh only by the restraining presence of another person at the moment of his cannibalistic temptation.

The novel's somber note is occasionally relieved by Sender's wry and grim humor, an ambivalent humor close to tears; the reader hardly ever laughs aloud, but winces while smiling inwardly. "In the army, on service, one is not asked if one has anything to complain of, one just has to obey orders. First you die, and then you can lodge your protest, if you like, 'in writing'" (107–8). The following is part of a description of the joviality and high spirits of the Spanish conscripts as they left their homes for military service, in bitter contrast with the inglorious return of those who did return: "Another soldier had stolen a chamber-pot and was wearing it on his head like an absurd helmet" (284).

During his nightmarish odyssey across the desert, Viance's suffering from thirst, hunger, exhaustion, and his wounds repeatedly reaches superhuman proportions and he becomes delirious. He sees only death and dead men all around him, and internally he is all but swallowed up by death. At these points the real and the unreal or merely imagined become confused and scenes cast a surrealistic aura over the narrative as when Viance repeatedly sees and hears a squadron of Spanish horsemen (184–85). Dreams and nightmares also contribute to the hallucinatory character of the narrative, and emphasize the intrinsic "message" of the work.

In his later works, notably in *The Sphere* which I shall discuss in Chapter 5, Sender tends to look "downward" to man's instinctive nature as the basis for the truly human rather than "upward" to what might be called a spiritual realm. In a broad sense his view is Pantheistic and he makes a great deal of what might be called the natural unity of all created objects. Viance "felt a love for the earth akin to the gratitude he had once felt toward the dead horse. But the love he felt was the natural, cosmic affinity of the earth to the earth. He hated no one" (225). Viance was beyond the ordinary passions of ordinary men and women, in a metaphysical realm where morality, as conventionally conceived, had no meaning. Earlier one dark night there had been "something in the character of the night that . . . inclined Viance to believe in some kind of justice that lived and breathed in the background of all he did and thought. A kind of bright and translucent justice implicit in all things" (112). Such musings serve as a counterweight to the demonic brutality of the novel besides impregnating it occasionally with a poetic-philosophical glow which adds interest and perspective.

As Carrasquer points out, Sender often realizes that Viance, a Spanish peasant, could not or would not express himself in such a philosophical vein; consequently he resorts to varied devices such as: "Viance did not elaborate [on] these reflections. But he had an obscure notion of their main outlines and they became rooted in his subconsciousness" (196); "We live, Viance thought obscurely" (229); "Viance, intuitively and vaguely conscious of all this, felt . . ." (225); and "Viance was ignorant of the full range of his intuitions and he was therefore unable to establish abstract conclusions" (225).

V. S. Pritchett, in 1934, wrote of the British edition that Sender's first novel has the interest of "uncovering the mind of the Spanish soldier-peasant" about the Moroccan defeat, and that "as literature the book has dignity but no great distinction."[6] *Pro Patria* is not a documentary novel, but it does have documentary value; it also has dignity and true distinction as literature. It is a story of death, death to the Spanish *pueblo,* physical and moral; the sacrifice of Spain's finest resource, its common people, upon the altar of the false patriotism and the economic interests of its ruling classes. In the end Viance breaks national boundaries, becoming a universal symbol of the common man as victim of injustice and man's inhumanity to man.

II Siete domingos rojos (Seven Red Sundays), 1932

It is significant that the subtitle of Sender's fourth novel, *Seven Red Sundays,* is *Novela de la prerrevolución española* (*Novel of the Spanish Pre-Revolution*). The book portrays an abortive proletarian uprising during seven days, seven "Sundays," in Madrid during the early days of the Spanish Republic, reflecting the author's intense involvement in revolutionary activities at the time, both as an observer and as a participant in the affairs of the CNT (Confederación Nacional de Trabajo, the National Federation of Labor). In substance and tone it recalls *O.P. (Orden Público) (O.P. [Public Order])*, 1931; *Viaje a la aldea del crimen (Trip to the Village of Crime)*, 1934; and *La noche de las cien cabezas (The Night of One Hundred Heads)*, 1934, three novels which Sender later (after the Civil War) has referred to as constituting a trilogy entitled *Términos del presagio (Terms of the Presage)*. Equally with the trilogy, *Seven Red Sundays* was an omen of the chaos of the coming Civil War. Apart from its literary merits the novel is of notable importance as a serious probing of the motives of the Spanish revolutionaries, an unveiling of the mind of the Spanish anarchists, syndicalists, communists, and socialists of the early thirties. Alfred Kazin and Philip Jordan have compared it with André Malraux's *La condition humaine (The Human Condition)*.[7]

Although the book is not to be taken as a historical record, it could have been written only by one who knew intimately the situation among the revolutionaries, the individuals involved and their viewpoints, the social problems of the proletariat, and the national political scene. Speaking of this time in his life, Sender said: "I was not in politics but I was involved with social problems, problems in which I did not fail also to see the literary and poetic side."[8] Though the work ostensibly portrays a general strike in Madrid, it is not to be regarded as a novelized reporting of a specific strike in Madrid or in some other Spanish city, but as an imaginative composite of the ferment among the workers of the cities of Spain during the first year of the Second Spanish Republic. Valle-Inclán has referred to it as a mural painting.[9]

It took courage to publish *Seven Red Sundays* in Spain in 1932; it was regarded by the Spanish Republicans as offensive, and it surely could not have been well received by either the socialists or communists. Outside of Spain its acceptance has been much more positive. Its English translation has appeared in two British editions and three American, and the novel has also appeared in Russian, Danish, Swedish, Czechoslovakian, and Dutch translations. The most recent American edition was in 1968; it is interesting that the basic attitude toward, and opposition to, the existing social order of the Spanish strikers in Sender's novel so strikingly parallel those of the more radical-ized student-strikers in American universities in the late sixties. Quotations below are from the English translation published in the United States in 1936.[10]

In the preface Sender asserts that his book is addressed not to the readers' intelligence, but to their sensibility. Disclaiming any political or moral purpose, he writes that he seeks only to transmit "the truth of a living humanity displayed in the convulsions of a Spanish revolutionary episode" (13). Admitting that the consequences of the upheaval are many, he insists that what interests him most is "a truth of the most generous kind" which lies behind anarcho-syndicalist dreams "of a strange state of society in which all men are as disinterested as St. Francis of Assisi, bold as Spartacus, and able as Newton and Hegel" (15). Some, not all, of Sender's anarchists in the novel are indeed noble dreamers and willing to risk all for their Utopian dreams; they are Don Quixotes dressed as workmen suffocating in an inhuman and unjust industrialized society.

As in *Pro Patria*, this novel has no real plot; it is merely the story (told from various perspectives) of what happened during the seven days of a proletarian uprising in Madrid, seven "Sundays" all red with blood. Trouble starts on the first day when Civil Guards break up a meeting of revolutionary workmen, killing three laborers in the fracas. In protest of the killing, the anarchists, syndicalists, and communists, later joined by the socialists, are able to institute a general strike. On the second "Sunday" street fighting erupts when the funeral procession for the workmen is attacked. Each of the subsequent four "Sundays" is also "red" with blood as sniping, sabotage, arrests, executions, police torture, and employment of the "Law of Flight" result until the movement is thoroughly suppressed. The seventh "Sunday" is one of aftermath and dejection for the strikers, although one feels that the real spirit behind the outbreak is stronger than ever—portending future evil. The book begins with a kind of prologue by comrade Villacampa, an anarchist and a participant in the strike, and closes with an epilogue by Samar, a young intellectual journalist and revolutionist; in between the novel is divided into seven sections, each corresponding to a "Sunday."

The strikers can be divided into four general groups: anarchists, syndicalists, communists, and socialists. The last-named were not regarded as revolutionaries although they, for the sake of temporary expediency, were cooperating in the strike; as collaborators with the new Republic, they were distrusted by the other strikers. Many anarchists were also members of syndicates; hence the term anarcho-syndicalist. The revolutionaries are unsuccessful in giving coherence and political purpose to their energetic efforts against the established social order. Within the anarchist ranks there is dissension between the old men and the young. The communists and the anarchists disagree radically as to the ends to be achieved by the uprising. Samar, who has fervently espoused the proletarian cause, realizes the futility of the revolution. He reflects: "The behavior of some of the comrades, . . . is against us. It is pushing us all down. Without meaning it, they are on the way to finish us all off, themselves and me" (265).

Despite, however, the book's intense probing of the inner motives of the revolutionaries, a balanced probing which reveals both the sublime and the ridiculous, the true and the false, the intelligent and the stupid among the strikers and Sender's disavowal of a moral purpose for it, *Seven Red Sundays* in its totality constitutes a clear affirmation of revolutionary values. Alongside its idealism, of course, the practical weaknesses of the revolution become abundantly clear. Samar, who obviously represents the author himself, says: "The intoxication of our multitudes is negative. It is not to be negotiated with. But many negatives may make an affirmative . . ." (312). Samar's mystical faith in the proletarian cause can be seen in passages such as the following:

Our protest is not charged with political formulas, but is a question of the future against the past which traditionalists wish to prolong. They are men of tradition, we of hope. All that we are doing accelerates disintegration, demoralizes the traditionalists and their traditions, brings up to the surface the hidden force, the living reserve of humanity which we represent, we who alone in the western world remain faithful to nature and identify ourselves with it. (272)

Manuel Béjar states that underlying the opposition between the bourgeoisie and the proletariat in *Seven Red Sundays* can be discerned Sender's peculiar classification of men, according to their inner motives or attitudes, into those who cultivate the "person" (mask, appearance) on the one hand, and those who are true to their *hombría* (man-ness or manhood, universal human essence) on the other.[11] To be *bourgeois,* in the lexicon of *Seven Red Sundays,* is although not expressly stated, to be a "person"—person; to be truly revolutionary is to be a free man of *hombría,* a "man"—man who is true to the human species. The revolutionaries represent "the living reserve of humanity"; they are the only ones in the Western world who "remain faithful to nature" and identify themselves with nature (272). "Things are so badly arranged in this dirty *bourgeois* world," complains Comrade Villacampa, "that we can't be natural" (221). To determine whether one is *bourgeois* or revolutionary, one must not look to groups but to individuals; among the "revolutionaries" the author reserves his sharpest satire for those whose motives and loyalties are more truly *bourgeois* than revolutionary; an example of these pseudo-revolutionaries is the well-to-do Argentine who associates with the revolution in the hope of gaining publicity as an anarchist, thereby hoping to win a certain respect from his *bourgeois* associates who until now have regarded him as merely stupid. The "person-man" dichotomy is only implicit in *Seven Red Sundays;* it is more explicitly developed two years later in *The Night of One Hundred Heads,* and further elaborated in *The Sphere.* In Chapter 5 I discuss the dichotomy in detail.

The atmosphere of crisis of the uprising is to some extent reflected in the very form of the novel. There is a constant shifting of narrative points of view, especially during the first half of the book, which may be disconcerting to some readers. A reviewer of the American edition of the novel complained: "Aesthetically as well as logically it would seem that social chaos should be simulated rather than reproduced."[12] The book opens with a prologue chapter in which comrade Villacampa speaks in the first person; in the second and third chapters an omniscient author narrates in the third person; in the fourth, Star, the fifteen- or sixteen-year-old daughter of one of the slain revolutionaries, narrates in the first person; in the fifth, the moon itself (as "Lady Moon") speaks her mind in the first person, followed by Samar the journalist in the sixth; an unknown representative of the Federation (the F.A.I., the Iberian Federation of Anarchists) in the seventh; Villacampa in the eighth; Samar in the ninth; and so on, although for the remainder of the thirty chapters the point of view of the omniscient author tends to prevail. Comments Alfred Kazin:

> By reflecting in the pattern of his narrative the actual confusion and excitement in their minds, Sender has given the masses a single character and the novel a collective drama. . . . In an effort to convey the psychology of the group, he has divided some of the principal emotions among individuals who are not characterized adequately; as a result, the emotions of some are not intelligible, and the turmoil supposed to be indicative of the group, or of its environment, becomes external to it—the looseness of the narrative reveals nothing, in these passages, but the looseness of the narrative.[13]

On balance it appears that though the novel's structure may have weakened the sharp delineation of characters, narrative thrust and other "novelistic elements," it has gained in other ways, in ways which are in consonance with the author's intention to communicate artistically "a human truth of the most generous kind" (15). Sender succeeds in capturing the atmosphere and the spirit of the revolution, imbuing it at times with a lyrical dimension. The root or the essence of the revolution seems to be what Samar calls "this longing to live which oppresses us and always will oppress us" (384). Theodore Purdy, Jr. concludes that "the book is literature, and gives us . . . a vivid impression of those illiterate workmen who are fighting for their dream of a juster society based on living realities."[14] F. T. Marsh writes: "The book is obviously sincere and illumined by a tortured and striving mind."[15]

Although *Seven Red Sundays* has no protagonist unless it be the collective one of the revolutionaries, one character, Samar, is given more space and attention than any of the others. He and the other main characters reveal themselves directly through their own narrations in the first person but also through dialogue, interior monologue, letters, evaluations by other characters, conversations with Star's pet rooster, with the moon, with a pair of underwear shorts, etc. Some characters may represent different aspects of the multifaceted revolution: Samar, the intellectual side; comrade Villacampa, the grocer's assistant, pure (or instinctive)anarchism; Star, the "child of the revolution," impulsive, uninhibited "direct action" (while the other comrades dispute endlessly, she *acts*); and Amparo, the lovely daughter of an army colonel who becomes involved in the suppression of the disorder, enlightened *bourgeoisie* sentimentalities, roughly what Samar calls spirit.

Embedded in the events of the seven days of the revolution is the story of Samar and his *bourgeois* sweetheart, Amparo. One is reminded of Pérez Galdós' technique of weaving into his historical novels, his *Episodios nacionales* (*National Episodes*), the private love story of one or more of his principal characters, although in Sender's novel the private story of Samar and Amparo takes on an allegorical meaning, thereby reinforcing the author's central intention in writing the book. At the beginning of the novel Samar is a divided man: he loves Amparo, who is the very incarnation of the best in the bourgeois world, and yet he loves the revolution. Precipitated by the events of the social upheaval, a polarization between the bourgeoisie and the proletariat occurs, and Samar finally resolves the dilemma in favor of the proletariat, feeling as he does that to yield to Amparo's love would be to allow himself to be seduced away from the world of living realities, to betray his truest self, and become lost in the false values of the *bourgeois* world.

Amparo, finding it impossible, despite her love, to adjust to Samar's world, commits suicide. In despair Samar realizes that in a real sense he had killed Amparo, the spirit of the *bourgeois* world. In an emotional scene Samar uncovers her body in the mortuary and bids her goodbye forever. Though Amparo's death is tragic and Samar's involvement in it might be seen as criminal, in the novel it comes to symbolize his "liberation" from the bourgeois "spirit." Though part of Samar dies, another part awakens with spontaneous joy. In prison he meditates in the book's epilogue: "Dreams for prison. The spirit for the mortuary. Life is in the streets and life is mechanical and materialistic" (434). To him the "spiritual world" of the *bourgeoisie* is false; the real secret of the universe is to be found by looking downwards, not upwards, by identifying oneself with material and feeling himself in unity with the physical world. At this level, he believes, the revolution finds its real inspiration.

Sender uses external or ordinary reality in *Seven Red Sundays* as a solid base of operations, as a kind of trampoline from which to launch his leaps to "higher" realities. The chapter in which the moon becomes a character is an example of unrestrained imagination which clearly violates the usual norms for a "realistic" work; the talking moon brings to mind the fantasies in *Paradox, Rey* (*Paradox, King*) by Pío Baroja. The "realism" of *Seven Red Sundays* is a strange fusion of ordinary reality with other "realities," imaginative "realities" that sometimes add an intellectual dimension, at others a lyrical or metaphysical overtone.

III Mr. Witt en el cantón (Mr. Witt Among the Rebels), *1936*

For *Mr. Witt en el cantón* (translated into English as *Mr. Witt Among the Rebels*), Sender was awarded first prize in Spain's National Literature Contest (novel section) for 1935 by a five-man jury, chaired by Antonio Machado and having as one of its members Pío Baroja. The National Prize was regarded at the time as the nation's highest literary award. The Civil War which followed upon the heels of the publication of *Mr. Witt Among the Rebels* (hereafter referred to as *Mr. Witt*) in 1936 abruptly suspended literary activity in Spain; consequently Sender's novel had insufficient time to be assimilated and fully appreciated by the Spanish literary world, as Francisco Carrasquer has pointed out.[16] Happily, its reprinting in Spain in 1968 made it once again available to Spanish critics and readers. It has been translated into English, Russian, Swedish, and Finnish.

According to its author, *Mr. Witt* poses the problem of the "erotic unconsciousness of man and of woman linked with the collective unconsciousness in the panorama of a revolution."[17] Primarily it is a novelized version of the struggle during the early days of the First Spanish Republic in 1873 when the province of Murcia with its headquarters in Cartagena attempted to separate from the central government in Madrid, and establish its own autonomy. The weaknesses (confusion, excessive individualism, inept leadership, unrealistic expectations, lack of discipline and cohesion, etc.) of the Murcian rebels are essentially the same as those which plagued the rebels in Sender's earlier novel, *Seven Red Sundays,* 1932, as well as those which soon after the appearance of the novel were to doom the Second Spanish Republic. The novel is divided into three books and twenty-one chapters; the events of the uprising from its beginning in March until its total suppression in December of 1873 are related in chronological order. In a manner reminiscent of the *Episodios nacionales* of Galdós, Sender fuses real events and real persons with events and creatures of his own invention into an artistic unity.

Mr. Witt, a slightly bald Victorian English gentleman of fifty-three and a consulting engineer in the naval arsenal at Cartagena, and his vivacious Spanish wife, Milagritos, thirty-five, are certainly among Sender's finest literary creations. They are characterized with consummate skill. Their story is intrinsically intermeshed with the broader scene of violent social unheaval. The contrast in character and temperament between Mr. Witt and Milagritos is sustained throughout the novel and becomes an admirable study in human psychology but never an end in itself, never divorced from the story of the revolution.

Mr. Witt is a highly civilized gentleman, an intelligent, book-collecting man of liberal views who believes in progress and justice, but who insists that they must come through science and in an orderly manner. A timid man, his thirst for adventure has been suppressed; fifteen years previously, in the only really adventurous act of his life, he had married the warm-blooded Milagritos. In contrast Milagritos is a nonreflective person who abandons herself to intuition or the "logic" of the passions; she is a natural woman who comes to represent Nature and primitive unruliness. The contrast between head and heart is deftly drawn, skillfully made incarnate in Mr. Witt and Milagritos. In the somber interior of their home, overlooking the naval harbor, the two have lived together in comparative contentment, although each blames the other for their childless condition. Events from the outside, the revolt, come to illuminate the differences between the two temperaments. Sustained also throughout the novel is an implicit dualism yet intimate connection between the "inside" world of Mr. Witt's private psychological drama and the catastrophic events occurring in the world outside.

As the revolution begins, its romance, adventure, and intense activity appeal powerfully to Milagritos. Joyfully and whole-heartedly she throws herself into the task of caring for the wounded; she looks younger and prettier as the days go by, despite the fact that the insurgents find their situation deterio-rating into utter hopelessness. All the while Mr. Witt undergoes a deep psychological conflict; an event which occurred five years previously (during the Glorious Revolution of 1868 against Queen Isabella II) returns to plague him. What now troubles Mr. Witt's conscience is that, had he acted more decisively, he could have saved Carvajal, a colorful revolutionary poet and a nephew of Milagritos (although she called him her cousin because of the similarity of their ages), from the firing squad. Was it because he had suspected Milagritos of having a roman-tic attachment to Carvajal? Knowing that the man who despises himself is lost, Mr. Witt becomes a psychological battleground. To justify his reprehensible conduct of five years earlier, he now suspects Milagritos of an attachment to two colorful leaders of the new uprising, Antonete Gálvez and Colau, men who are intimately identified, in Mr. Witt's mind, with the dead poet. He grows increasingly uncommunicative with his wife; eventu-ally his gnawing remorse and suspicions lead him to become the accomplice in an attempt to destroy Colau by setting fire to the frigate which he commands.

In the end the cantonalists, hemmed in by land and by sea, are utterly crushed although hostilities have not yet ceased when the book concludes. Although she knows of her husband's perfidious conduct, Milagritos secures for him a safe-conduct certificate that will permit the Witts to leave Cartagena. Realiz-ing that her husband's betrayal of the revolution by attempting to have Colau destroyed was motivated by jealousy, a jealousy that confirms his love for her, rather than by political or ideologi-cal reasons, Milagritos is able, as Francisco Carrasquer has stated, to forgive her husband his actions and to resume normal rela-tions with him.[18] She still hopes to have a child from her mar-riage. As the couple leaves for Madrid, Mr. Witt suggests that they go on to London and never return, but Milagritos flashes back at him that she (and by implication he also) will return to Cartagena after the establishment of peace.

The narrative point of view is that of an omniscient author. The story is unified around two poles: Mr. Witt and the revolution. Scenes shift from inside the Englishman's cozy home, symbolic of Mr. Witt's isolation, to the great outside world where catastrophic events transpire, events which are at times observed by Mr. Witt from the balcony of his house. The "street" enters his home daily with the return of Milagritos from her activities as a medical aide. With an admirable economy of words Sender achieves a well-rounded impression of the revolution—its leaders, its proletarian flavor, its confusion, its weaknesses, its enthusiasms, its brutality and suffering, its heroism and greatness of spirit. Its realism is almost total. Mr. Witt the Englishman gives to the novel a note of detached objectivity which acts as a counterweight to what might otherwise have emerged as an excessively subjective portrayal of a popular uprising. Writes V. S. Pritchett: "*Mr. Witt* is a far better book [than *Seven Red Sundays*]. It is serene and accomplished, a novel of a very high order, purged of the provincial weaknesses of the earlier volume."[19] The Spanish critic Eugenio de Nora comments:

From the aesthetic point of view, as we have already indicated, *Mr. Witt* is a novel which approaches perfection, balanced in its elements, alternately tight and relaxed in its psychological analyses, suggestive in its evocations, fluid and exciting in reflecting the dynamic nature of the historical situation, clean and plastic in establishing the profile and the color of each scene; moreover, in the perspective of Spanish narrative literature during the decade of the thirties (a perspective not so sterile as usually believed) it is a fundamental link—and perhaps the nearest one—to the sensibility that was to prevail.[20]

IV   *Minor Novels*

A.   El Verbo se hizo sexo (The Word Became Sex)

In 1931 Sender published *El Verbo se hizo sexo (Teresa de Jesús)* (*The Word Became Sex [Theresa of Jesus]*),[21] a novelized biography of St. Theresa, although it could also be classified as a historical novel. If we can believe the author's own words, it was written when he was a lad of fifteen or sixteen years,[22] and is therefore probably the first book that he wrote. In a letter dated December 1, 1966, to Francisco Carrasquer, Sender wrote: "As far as St. Theresa is concerned I should like for you to forget *The Word Became Sex* (a sin of my childhood) and readjust your opinions to the impression you receive from reading *Tres novelas teresianas* (*Three Theresan Novels*) that Destino is going to publish (before the end of the year). I have suppressed the *Word* from the list of my works and these three short novels will take its place."[23] Although repudiated by its author, *The Word* must remain as a Senderian novel; it is expressive of the author's interest in the Saint of Avila during his youth while the later book, *Three Theresan Novels*, expresses that same interest but from the perspective of his advanced maturity—thirty-six years, 1931 to 1967, separate the publication dates of the two works with probably more than forty-five years between their times of composition. Sender's fascination and admiration for Theresa began in adolescence (while a student in Reus, he once wrote) and has persisted into his old age.

The title of the novel was chosen deliberately for its "shock" value. Had he simply entitled it *Saint Theresa of Jesus,* he writes in its prologue, it would have evoked no more in the minds of the bourgeois public than "an image of wood festooned in gold and laced handkerchiefs."[24] The title may indeed have had a scandalizing effect, but it may have repelled more readers than it attracted. It apparently aroused little attention. Homero Serís accused the book of contradictions and of sounding "a bit hollow," concluding that "One can well dispense with the reading of this book."[25]

The title is indeed inaccurate, for Sender himself explains that he does not believe in the "Word" (in theology, Jesus Christ or the Holy Spirit). Sender's thesis seems to be that in the case of Theresa physical sex became sublimated into "love" or "spirit," just the opposite of what is implied in the book's title. In effect, a materialistic explanation for the Saint's mysticism is implied though not developed. "Sex is to mysticism what the heart is to romanticism."[26] Yet Sender does not seek to explain away the supernatural in the Saint's life through appealing to modern psychology or to science. As for Freud, he dismisses him with: "Freud would believe himself capable of tearing St. Theresa apart and explaining her, but what is most probable is that the Saint would make him look ridiculous. Science can never see beyond half of a genius, as it sees no more than half of life."[27] Although rejecting an orthodox Catholic or biblical belief in the supernatural, Sender has at the same time distrusted science as the only valid means to penetrate the mysterious and the irrational or even as the best way for such penetration; on the contrary he has insisted on the primacy of natural intuition.

In its notes of retroactive social protest the novel is typical of Sender; the social climate and historical reality of the period are well recreated through the story of Theresa and her family. A heavy reliance is made on dialogue, and there are occasional passages of poetic prose of high literary quality.

B. O.P. (Orden público) (O.P. [Public Order])

O.P. (Orden público) (*O.P. [Public Order]*),[28] published in 1931 (reprinted in Mexico in 1941), was the first of three Senderian novels which the author, from a post-Civil War perspective, named the *Términos del Presagio* (*Terms of the Presage*) trilogy.[29] The other two books of the series are: *Viaje a la aldea del crimen* (*Trip to the Village of Crime*) and *La noche de las cien cabezas* (*The Night of One Hundred Heads*), both published in 1934.

These novels, according to Sender, are an expression "rather direct and concrete—rather substantial, of a time that was critical for the immediate future of Spain,"[30] and form a presage "dull or clever, simple or brilliant" of events which followed their publication.[31] Sender considers them living records of "the Spain that we lived then [the decade of 1926-1936], and of the Spain that lived in the author,"[32] written when the catastrophe of the Civil War was being incubated in Spanish life. Almost two decades later, Sender sought to incorporate the essence of the three works into *El verdugo afable* (*The Affable Hangman*), 1952.[33]

O.P. (Public Order), inspired by the author's experiences as a political prisoner for three months in 1927 in Madrid's Model Jail, has no plot; it merely relates in a haphazard manner—reminiscent of Baroja—of what the Journalist (Sender) observed and experienced during his imprisonment. The narrative point of view shifts from the Journalist to that of the Wind to that of an omniscient author. The reader is introduced to a motley and gruesome array of prison characters: shyster lawyers, homosexuals, a man who had committed murder in order to gain recognition for having done an "important" act; inspector Alarm; a benign official, etc.

One day, because of a collective protest against the bread served to the prisoners, the Journalist, along with the others who had participated in the complaint, is thrown into solitary confinement for a number of days. There in pitch darkness, he communes with the wind—which becomes the Wind, symbolizing eternity, transcendental truth. Explains the author: "In jail one becomes drunk with eternity and can do no less than be sincere and deep."[34] The Wind laments over the social and economic ulcer which is Spain. The Wind—Absolute Justice—Sender implies, is on the side of the political prisoners incarcerated under the regime of Primo de Rivera. "The Wind was a political prisoner. *O.P.* But the Wind continued in the field, in the street, in the hair of a little girl, and on the wing of a stork."[35]

The Wind (still young—only two and one-half eternities old) possesses, according to the author, a very rich treasure of accumulated experiences. It counsels the Journalist: "Don't worry. Although you are here within the prison, your voice goes with me and enters everywhere. They have also wanted to shut me up like you."[36] The philosophic substance of *Public Order* is obviously that though individual men may be imprisoned, the eternal spirit can never be—men may kill idealists, but ideals never die. The mills of the gods may grind slowly, but they grind surely. Man may, if he chooses, unite his voice to the voice of eternal truth—the Wind.

As a novel *Public Order* is second rate, its literary quality uneven. With the exception of the Journalist, none of the prisoners seems to be a living person. Real narrative drive is lacking. The author's method is more descriptive than narrative, more subjective than objective, and there is little humor. The book does, however, succeed in communicating vividly what has been felt by Sender during his imprisonment. As testimonial literature of a phase of Spanish life it is noteworthy.

C.   Viaje a la aldea del crimen (Trip to the Village of Crime)

In February of 1934 Sender published *Trip to the Village of Crime*,[37] a novelized version of the peasant uprising and its brutal repression by Government assault guards in the Andalusian village of Casas Viejas a year earlier, January 10, 1933. Sender had visited Casas Viejas immediately after the uprising and, in a series of articles published in *La Libertad*, a Madrilian newspaper, he had strongly criticized the handling of the situation by President Manuel Azaña's administration; the articles were later collected and published as a short book, *Casas Viejas*, 1933.[38] *Trip to the Village of Crime* is based both on the articles and some additional material.

Although noteworthy for its lucid and flowing style, *Trip to the Village of Crime* is valuable primarily as an exposé of feudalistic conditions prevailing in rural Spain in modern times; Don Ramón saw the Andalusian agrarian problem basically as a struggle between "feudal" landlords and the landless day laborers.

D.   La noche de las cien cabezas (The Night of One Hundred Heads)

The third member of the triad of novels which Sender later baptized as the *Terms of the Presage* trilogy is *La noche de las cien cabezas* (*The Night of One Hundred Heads*), 1934.[39] Its subtitle, *Novela del tiempo en delirio* (*Novel of Time in Delirium*), suggests its tendency to fantasy and allegory. Juan L. Alborg calls it an "allegorical fantasy, conceptual and satirical, that has as much of the biting scorn of *El Criticón* [the masterpiece of Baltasar Gracián, the Aragonese Jesuit writer of moral treatises, 1601-1648] as of the variegated and impudent imagination of Quevedo's *Visions,* which in many passages it resembles."[40] Its caricature of members of Spanish society also brings to mind the painter Goya.

One cold, winter night Evaristo the Frog (so called because he had made his living by selling frogs to a medical laboratory) finds refuge in a niche in the wall of a cemetery in the outskirts of Madrid. There in the cold of the night he died while a revolutionary cyclone strikes Madrid, sweeping up in its path a vast human cargo among which it deposits in the cemetery one hundred heads of people representing a cross section of Spanish society. As each head lands in the cemetery, it becomes the occasion for satirical commentary upon Spanish life as well as philosophical speculation as to the meaning of life and death. In the end the revolutionary tempest ceases and in a phantasmagorical scene workmen erect a dolmen, a monument not to Pascual, their comrade who has fallen, the implication is, in a battle with the guardians of the existing social order, but to undifferentiated man or *hombría* ("man-ness"). The implication through this act and others in the book is that the cult of one's personality, the singularization of the individual, must give way in the new society to communist ideals, to the subordination of the individual to the collectivity, a theme which Sender has continued to develop in various books and especially in *The Sphere*.

Although *The Night of One Hundred Heads* presents a brilliant and penetrating vision of Spanish life and contains most of Sender's favorite themes, it falls short as a novel. Except for the first two of its twenty-eight chapters it has little narrative interest. Characterization is almost exclusively fragmentary caricature. Alborg refers to it as "living satire that is disguised by the clothing of a novel."[41]

CHAPTER 4

Aragon in Retrospect: Three Novels

I   El lugar de un hombre (A Man's Place), *1939*

IN *A Man's Place,* Sender has imaginatively recreated life in a sleepy Aragonese town in the early part of this century. The town itself, Ontiñena, is, as stated in Chapter 1 of this study, easily recognized from the description of its physical setting as Alcolea de Cinca where the author spent his early childhood. Although the work begins as a first-person narrative by a sixteen-year-old youth, obviously Sender himself, its point of view becomes at times indistinguishable from that of an omniscient author.

Rather exceptional for Senderian novels, *A Man's Place* has a close-knit and clearly worked out plot. Nicholson B. Adams asserts that it "is more perfectly constructed than Sender's other works, and gives an admirable picture of a whole village which is terribly upset when a man supposedly murdered is suddenly found: an excellent study in human relationships."[1] Page references in parentheses are from the excellent English translation by Oliver La Farge, *A Man's Place* (New York, 1940).

The story opens when Sabino García Illeras, a former resident of Ontiñena who had been declared murdered by two workmen sixteen years previously, is found and "captured" by a hunting party in the desert plateau which rises back of Ontiñena. Sabino is thus restored to his "place" in human society.

Having related Sabino's reappearance and the circumstances surrounding it, the author goes back in time to reconstruct Sabino's life before his disappearance, and to tell of the events which resulted from his disappearance. As a boy Sabino worked long hours collecting manure and then selling it as fertilizer. His father was the village common-herder—"the man chosen for that is almost always good for nothing else" (71)—and his mother was a gleaner. Under the cruel jibes of his neighbors, his sense of inferiority grew, and in time socially he "ceased to exist" (74); he became a nobody, hardly possessing his own elemental manhood. For a brief while he found some compensations for his ignominious state in marriage but when his wife, Adela, proved to be an unfaithful slut, all faith in humanity seemed to desert him, and he simply disappeared into the backlands to live alone, living off the land like an animal.

Sabino was last seen in the presence of two laborers, Juan and Vicente, from the neighboring town of Castelnovo, a stronghold of the Liberals. Don Jacinto, the richest man in Ontiñena and the leader of the Conservatives as well as "the best friend the Civil Guard had in that part of the country" (100), saw in Sabino's disappearance an opportunity to make political capital. Accordingly, the two laborers who had been seen drinking with Sabino at a crossroads tavern ("tradition held that it was at crossroads that crimes were committed" [101]) were charged by the Civil Guard with murdering Sabino for the wages he had just received. Sender's realism is at its poignant best in the harrowing scenes of torture which follow until finally, totally broken in body and spirit, the laborers confess to their "crime." Unable to produce Sabino's corpse, they are led further to lie and to declare that they had fed the dead body to the pigs. They are sentenced to life imprisonment in the prison in Lérida; fifteen years later, because of good behavior, they are released and return to Castelnovo a few months before their supposed victim, Sabino, reappears. Their "crime" had thoroughly discredited the Liberals in their town, and the Conservatives assumed political control in Castelnovo, as Don Jacinto had foreseen they would. The acceptable "truth" throughout the region and until the return of Sabino was that "Juan and Vicente, demoralized by Liberal ideas, had put Sabino to death to rob him" (146). All of the plans of the Liberals, "no matter how harmless, ran up against the same wall—the crime" (134).

Vicente is able, somehow or other, to resume life with his wife and reestablish himself in the life of his village; Juan, however, survives only long enough to be vindicated by the reappearance of Sabino. The wrong done the laborers can never be undone. Sabino, however, finds a better life awaiting him in society; his return becomes a political issue, an opportunity for the Liberals to avenge themselves by accusing the Conservatives of the injustices done to Juan and Vicente. Justice demands retribution, and in the end the Liberals regain their power. As a symbol Sabino determines the local balance of political power; he becomes a kind of hero to the peasants. When Juan dies as a result of his sufferings, "the peasants burned another of Don Jacinto's haystacks" (254). Later they burn his farm, Los Pinos, with its thousand-year-old trees. These actions may be interpreted as the first faint rumblings of a coming revolution against an unjust social system, perhaps even of the Spanish Civil War.

Under the impact of being regarded as "somebody" for the first time in his life, Sabino's personality begins to expand. The town council votes to give him a respectable position as a guard in the Irrigation Syndicate at a salary "on which he could live like a king" (260). With a new sense of social worth, he is able to wait patiently and with dignity for his wife to separate peacefully from the man whom she had married during his absence and to return to him. He even evinces a moral sense, something impossible in his former degraded state, and asks Juan to forgive him for having occasioned him so much evil.

"What have you done, Sabino?" the commandant [of the ditch guard] asked him.
"The least a man can do. I went away. Isn't that what I have legs for, to go where I want to?" (280)

Sender's deep faith in the value of man *simply because he is man* is nowhere more clearly seen than in *A Man's Place*. In the "Brief Notice" at the front of the original Spanish edition of the novel, Sender declares his purpose: "In this book is my sentiment of what is human and perhaps the root of the only revolutionary humanism possible. . . . man's place appears empty and that emptiness determines the value of absence, which, after all, is nothing more than the 'countervalue' of presence."[2] The novel is a parable of the human condition. Sabino is representative man; the upheavals attendant upon both his absence from society and his subsequent return to that society suggest that, despite appearances, man—individual man—is of transcendental importance. To deny him his rightful "place" in life is to tempt the fates. Writes

Sherman H. Eoff in a brilliant study of *A Man's Place* in one chapter of his book, *The Modern Spanish Novel*: "Sender begins at rock bottom in the examination of his subject by subtracting a person's presence from the world of human relations and then observing the consequences of both his absence and his reappearance. It is an existentialist approach in that it proposes to deal with human reality entirely within the precincts of a person's mere 'being here.'"[3] Though specific evils in the Spanish social structure are revealed in the novel, the work must be taken also as an indictment of man's inhumanity to man in general.

The style is simple; direct narration (with a minimum of description, secondary characters, and commentary) recreates vividly the scenes and flavor of the Spanish milieu in which the action occurs.

II Crónica del alba (Chronicle of Dawn), *1942*

The best known of Sender's novels among students of Spanish in American universities is *Crónica del alba* (*Chronicle of Dawn*) which first appeared as a separate novel, and was later to become the first of the nine "novels" incorporated into the three-volume series bearing the same title. The remaining eight "novels" or parts of the series are to be discussed briefly in Chapter 7, "Other Novels, 1939–1971." The Spanish school-text edition of *Chronicle of Dawn,* edited by Sender's wife, was published in 1946. Having undergone numerous reprintings, it has continued to be widely used in undergraduate classes of Spanish.[4]

In a preface entitled "Aunque no lo parezca" ("Unlikely As It May Seem"), Sender purports to explain how *Chronicle of Dawn* came to be written. His intimate friend, José Garcés, a thirty-six-year-old Spanish Republican army officer, lies ill in a prison camp in France during the closing days of the Spanish Civil War. As long as the Republic still holds out, Don José continues studying a technical manual of fortifications. Once, however, news of the total defeat of the Republic arrives, his very life-principle is destroyed. He throws away the manual and wants only to die, explaining: "We lost and we must pay. Our war was an undertaking to win or die."[5]

But before leaving the prison camp "by the only door worthy of us [Loyalist officers]," he feverishly writes an autobiography

of his childhood days, saying that it helps him "to remain a man
of substance."[6] "In a man," he explains, "substance is faith."[7] Before dying José Garcés fills three notebooks which he gives to
Sender, who now offers them to the public "as they were, without
even dividing them into chapters. . . ."[8] In reality, of course, the
entire series is an autobiographical novel covering Sender's life
from age ten until well into the Civil War, the "midday" of his
life, although the first part or novel which we are now consider-
ing covers only his eleventh year. It is significant that Garcés is
the maiden name of the author's mother, and José is his own
middle name as well as his father's name.

By means of the indirect device of making José Garcés the
supposed author of the book and by the implied contrast of José's
grandiose dreams of his "dawn" with the cruel and dark realities
of his "midday" (at age thirty-six), one gets, writes Marjorie
Farber, "the whole monstrous discrepancy between the human
potential and the inhuman mechanized result: the love perverted
or corrupted, the courage exploited, the nobility thrown away."[9]
Essentially *Chronicle*, especially in the three novels of the first
volume, is a study in the origins of idealism. It is in childhood
and youth that ideals and dreams find easy acceptance and fulfill a central role in the development of the individual. Ideals
perhaps have their purest and fullest meaning at that time. They
were the same ideals which, in Sender's view, led him and others
to risk everything in the defense of the Spanish Republic. At the
same time, it is the story of his discovery of love, and of his
awakening to his rich cultural heritage. Love and idealism are
hardly distinguishable in Sender; ultimately they merge into one.

In one long chapter which constitutes the book except for its
prefatory remarks, José Garcés (now called Pepe) narrates in
the first person his adventures during his eleventh year of life
as the son of middle-class parents in a small rural Aragonese
town, probably a composite of Alcolea de Cinca and Tauste, the
two towns in which Sender lived as a young lad. Pepe possesses
an amazingly spacious ego and imagination. He begins: "When
I became ten years old I thought I had entered the period of
responsibilities. I began to take less part in street fights, in our
gang wars. I had a gang of my own in our town—eight or ten
boys . . . my parents [began] making it more and more difficult

for me to have a 'private' life."[10] The novel is a series of episodes told as memories of José Garcés, who jumps from one incident to another without strict regard for chronological order. The narrative is unified around Pepe's awakening personality. There are also progress and unity in the lad's growing love for his sweetheart, Valentina, in his increasing awareness of his heritage as a Spaniard, and of his responsibilities in life. Pepe appears to the reader as a real person, albeit a very unusual and heroic one. Indeed, the book's greatest charm lies in its characterization of Pepe. His conflicts with his father, a recurrent theme in Sender's work, are carefully drawn. In a sense, his father represents to the boy the impure and uncomprehending adult world, while the young are still uncontaminated and can see the truth.

One day in Mass Pepe kneels beside Valentina, the daughter of the local notary. Finding in his prayer book a section entitled "Words of God to the Enamoured Soul," he shows it to Valentina and says:

"I am God and you are the Enamoured Soul."
"Yes, I," she repeated slowly, "am the Enamoured Soul."[11]

The two then read alternately the parts corresponding to the "Enamoured Soul" and to "God." Reading one passage Valentina addresses her young lover as "Lord of love, of wisdom, and of power."[12] Hearing himself thus called "Lord of love, of wisdom, and of power" leaves Pepe confused and with a feeling of "a strange greatness."[13] Later, in a moment of confidence, he tells his tutor, Mosén Joaquín, an understanding and very human priest, that he is—to one person, Valentina, at least—"the Lord of love, of wisdom, and of power." The good priest counsels him: "I do not doubt it, my son. But every man must make himself worthy of his own thoughts of himself. I mean he must work, he must develop the gifts which God has given him."[14]

The major substance of the book is found in Pepe's efforts "to make himself worthy of his own thoughts of himself," to live up to his ideal of himself, to realize himself. From the time that he aspired to fulfill in some measure Valentina's high expectations of him, he devotes himself wholeheartedly to his studies—something which all the threats and whippings of his father had failed to do. In the examinations taken in Zaragoza he does very well, and feels that he is now the lord of wisdom. By his success as a gang leader and as a lover of Valentina he assumes that he has also become, at least in some degree, the lord of power and of love.

Roughly the last third of the novel relates Pepe's adventures while on a summer vacation with his family at the castle of Sancho Garcés. In a subterranean passage to the castle Pepe discovers several sheets of parchment, the preface to the ordinances made by the medieval ruler of the castle, Sancho Garcés, written in Latin. The document classifies the men most needed to insure the greatness of Spain into three groups: saints, poets, and heroes.

The three sorts of men, then, most necessary to establish greatness are saints, poets, and heroes. A land can be very rich without these virtues but it will not achieve greatness. . . . There are some who have more than one of these qualities, but it is enough for each of us to have one only, because if we possess it utterly, as God desires that men should possess things, then there can be no true saint without a touch of the poet, nor, finally any of the three without some of the virtues of others.[15]

We find a parallel here with Pepe's desire to be lord of love (saint), of wisdom (poet), and of power (hero). One also recalls Charles Baudelaire's great men: the priest, the poet, and the soldier.

One evening after Mosén Joaquín has read aloud his translation of the parchment to the Garcés family and visitors, a lively discussion on Spain's greatness ensues. Pepe's father sees Spain's greatness in her history, but others, including Pepe's mother and Mosén Joaquín, insist that "true greatness never dies. The source of it continues in other channels."[16] Mosén Joaquín, as if in ecstasy, declares:

"Oh, if we would dare to be what we all, more or less, are within ourselves!"

"What do you believe that we are?" asked the doctor.

"Heroes or saints or poets. Each of us is born with one of those seeds in his heart."[17]

Later Pepe becomes lost in the maze of underground passages under the castle and, in hallucinatory scenes, meets and talks with the ghosts of a poet, a saint, and a hero, all who have long since unjustly been put to death. Pepe is beginning to learn that living up to his ideal of greatness may well cost him his life. Soon after returning home with his family, he fights the neighborhood bully for having cruelly killed a beggar's dog. The outcome of this incident is his father's decision to send Pepe immediately to a monastery school at Reus. Before leaving, Pepe, remembering a dream he had in which he, a hero, was killed, asks Mosén Joaquín, his friend and champion, why heroes are killed. The priest replies: "These things are too deep for you to understand. But you once asked me what the word 'immolation' meant. That is it. There is the answer. You are impressed by that parchment we read. The end not only of heroes but of poets and of saints is thus, almost always. . . . Remember that word 'immolation.' "[18] Alone in his room at the boarding school, Pepe recalls his adventures in the castle. Heroes, saints, and poets were killed. Would he be killed? "If I am killed," he says to himself, "what of it. Now I understand immolation. I shall write and tell Mosén Joaquín. But it was a lie, I understood nothing.

"That came much later."[19] Thus the book ends.

This first part of the *Chronicle* series is one of Sender's best novels. Its vision of life, seen through the imagination of Pepe, achieves a lyrical and very human dimension. Its sense of life is austere, yet balanced with elements of dry humor. The realistic and the romantic find a balance. "Like all good tales of youth . . . ," writes Bertram Wolfe, "this tightly constructed and beautifully realized novel is lyrical, nostalgic, suffused with pathos and humor, but never on any account condescending, as are those false works based on the notion that the adult world is possessed of superior truth."[20] José R. Marra-López calls it "one of the best works of our contemporary literature."[21]

III Réquiem por un campesino español
(Requiem for a Spanish Peasant), 1953

Although set in an Aragonese village, *Requiem* is not part of the *Chronicle of Dawn* series. There are two planes of action in

Requiem. On the primary plane, the action of the present, almost nothing external happens. A village priest, Mosén Millán, sits in an armchair in the sacristy of his church, waiting to say a Requiem Mass for one of his parishioners, Paco el del Molino (Frank, the One from the Mill), murdered a year before by Fascist agents at the village cemetery in the early days of the Spanish Civil War. While anxiously waiting for people to arrive for the Mass, the priest reviews in his memory the entire life of the deceased villager, Paco. Though Mosén Millán does not really admit to himself his guilt, he is obviously troubled by a guilty conscience. Through a combination of weakness, ignorance, and intimidating circumstances, he had unwittingly betrayed Paco into the hands of his murderers. By volunteering to offer this Requiem Mass he is obviously seeking to quiet the suppressed but accusing voices rising from his subconscious mind.

The waiting period, the time of the first plane of the novel's action, takes about twenty minutes. Throughout this time, while remembering Paco's life, the priest surfaces intermittently to the present only to ask anxiously of the altar boy whether anybody has yet arrived, or nervously to greet the three richest men of the village, Paco's enemies and the ones most responsible for his murder. One by one these men enter the sacristy, each offering to pay for the Mass and each in turn being curtly refused by the priest. Each time that Mosén Millán returns fleetingly to the present from the past, the altar boy recites a fragment of a ballad anonymously composed by the villagers on the life and death of Paco, sometimes aloud and sometimes only to himself, or the priest himself recalls a fragment. Finally the boy excitedly reports that a mule has entered the sanctuary. The "mule," which turns out to be Paco's colt, is chased out of the church by the three rich men with the aid of the sexton. Mosén Millán then, after another memory flashback which narrates the final events in Paco's life, wearily drags himself from his armchair, walks into the chancel, and begins the Mass. Except for this movement his physical immobility is almost absolute. Only Paco's three enemies and the altar boy hear the Mass. Even as the priest performs the ritual he again remembers Paco's dying words, words of stunned surprise and reproach: "Mosén Millán." "A year had passed since all this had happened, but it seemed like a century. Yet Paco's death was so recent and fresh that Mosén Millán still thought he had bloodstains on his clothes."[22] The absence of the villagers at the Mass and the entrance of Paco's colt in the sanctuary represent the mute and animal-like protest of the people against the crime committed against Paco, who comes to be not only an individual but to symbolize the people (*el pueblo*) themselves. The narrative point of view for this first plane of action is that of an omniscient author writing in the third person.

On the second plane of action, the past, the point of view is that seen through the memories of the priest, although such a point of view is not totally maintained, since the hand of the author at times subtly replaces that of the priest. The action (on both planes) occurs in a nameless Aragonese village located near the Lérida border. The time encompassed by the second plane of action is that of Paco's lifetime of about twenty-six years plus the one year since his death in the beginning days of the Spanish Civil War in 1936—that is, from about 1910 to 1937, with special concentration around the final days of the Monarchy in the Spring of 1931 and the beginning of the Civil War. Mosén Millán's memories for the most part chronologically reconstruct Paco's life, beginning with his baptism and the celebration afterwards, followed by his early childhood, adolescence, courtship and marriage, his election to the village council, his involvement in opposing the feudal system of handholding, and finally his unjust death before a firing squad because of his involvement in socioeconomic reforms. Minor breaks in chronological order occasioned by free association of ideas help preserve the freshness and realism of the priest's memories, and do not detract from the superb compactness and economy of the narration.

Mosén Millán's vivid reconstruction of scenes from Paco's life in which he, as village priest, participated provides a memorable picture of the life and customs in a Spanish village during the first half of this century. Though not at all a *costumbrista* work, its vivid portrayal of Spanish life led William Jassey to use the novel in his doctoral thesis: "A Handbook for Teaching Spanish Civilization Through Ramón Sender's *Réquiem por un campesino español* as Selected Literature in the First Term of Fourth-Year Spanish in High School."[23] An integral part of this sociocultural scene is Paco, a product of his heredity and environment.

Paco had become an altar boy at about age seven. One day he accompanies the priest to a cave outside the village in which a poor man lies dying, accompanied only by his wife. This experience awakens in him a concern for human justice. His observation of Mosén Millán's actions while administering extreme unction as well as the priest's unsatisfactory answers to his questions about abject poverty in the village eventually lead to the boy's loss of interest in the Church and to his progressive separation from the priest's influence, although he maintains a friendship with, and regard for, Mosén Millán until the time of his assassination.

During the last days of the Monarchy and right after his marriage, Paco is elected village councilman along with other young men anxious for abolition of the feudal landholding system which prevailed in that area of Spain. The three richest men, all large landholders and one of whom also administers the lands for the absentee Duke, are upset. Paco is successful in leading the fight to obtain the free use of the Duke's lands by the villagers. His plans to alleviate grinding poverty in the village are also succeeding when one day in July (of 1936, no doubt) the Civil Guard is called away. Soon pistol-wielding young toughs from Madrid arrive and begin a reign of terror by killing selected villagers, including four councilmen, under cover of darkness, while the villagers stand by dumbly and helplessly. Paco escapes to an abandoned house in the country. The Duke's lands are restored to him. Don Valeriano, one of the three rich men, is made mayor. Mosén Millán is confused and further confuses the countryfolk by appearing in public with Don Valeriano, thus appearing to approve of the new turn of events. Almost his only action is to protest that some of the murdered peasants were not given an opportunity for confession.

The newcomers rapidly consolidate their position. In a conversation with Paco's father the priest learns where Paco is hiding. The pistol-wielding strangers put pressure upon Mosén Millán who, in a weak moment, reveals the whereabouts of Paco, though only after receiving a promise from their leader (who is called the "centurion" in the ballad, an obvious suggestion of the Roman Army which crucified Christ) that Paco would not be killed. When Paco resists capture by wounding two of the *señoritos* (dandies) sent to take him, the priest intercedes with the peasant, pleading with him to surrender, and assuring him that he would be tried before a court and perhaps go to jail, but "nothing more." Nevertheless, on the very day of his surrender Paco is marched to the village cemetery and summarily shot, along with two other villagers. Mosén Millán hears his last confession, and administers final rites. The Civil War is never once mentioned, but it is clear that *Requiem* is a faithful synthesis of what happened in not just one Spanish village, but in hundreds during that most frightful of struggles.

Contrary to what Robert Duncan states in his introduction to the school-text edition of *Requiem* (printed under its original title, *Mosén Millán*),[24] the book is a clear denunciation of the Church. Bernice Duncan writes:: "Never has the author's true religious faith and divergence from 'organized' religion been clearer than in this stinging condemnation of the clergy."[25] Robert Duncan is also mistaken in writing that Mosén Millán "integrated in his environment, is a man before anything else."[26] According to Sender's dichotomy "man-person" (to be discussed in Chapter 5), "man" is the imperishable human essence and the source of inspiration and heroism, while his "person" is the mask that he wears. Obviously the priest is a man whose long years of unthinking submission to the Church has slowly and subtly eroded his *hombría* or "man-ness," while his "person" or mask has grown stronger. He has become an organization man, more "priest" than "man," a "person"-man who can hardly help himself when he puts institutional interests before basic human values and betrays an innocent man into the hands of his murderers. The leaders of the Jewish Church acted in the same way toward Christ. Cedric Busette has published a short article which convincingly establishes Paco as a Christ figure.[27]

Paco is both an individual victim and a symbol of the Spanish people sacrificed in the Civil War. His spirit lives on. The penultimate sentence in the novel finds him, like Christ, present during the Mass: "He [the priest] thought he heard his name on the lips of the dying man, fallen to the ground: '...Mosén Millán.' "[28] "He dies physically," writes Cedric Busette, "but for Ramón Sender, his spirit must forever haunt the conscience of Spain as the unrealized possibility of rebirth."[29]

Requiem is a superbly written short novel, or novelette. Its tone throughout is sober and subdued. Its unity is almost absolute. Its style is straightforward narrative and lucid. Its portrayal of Spanish village life is memorable and accomplished with surprising economy. Its humor, the rough humor of the country folk it portrays, is noteworthy and contributes balance and spice. Its psychological realism in the characterization of Mosén Millán is the work of a man who deeply knows human nature. The periodic interpolation of fragments from the ballad is like a musical counterpoint to the priest's tortured memories, and together with those memories (in which past and present fuse) creates a third plane of time, an atemporal one, writes Peñuelas.[30] Through the ballad a mythical dimension to the story becomes visible.

CHAPTER 5

The Sphere: *The Final "What" of Things*

IN 1969 Sender published in Madrid the definitive edition of
his most serious novel, *La esfera* (*The Sphere*), a symbolic
and poetic-philosophical work. Without question "it holds the
key to the understanding of Sender's fundamental perspective
on himself and on his universe."[1] The first edition of *The Sphere*
had appeared in Mexico thirty years earlier with the title *Proverbio de la muerte* (*Proverb of Death*), 1939. In 1947 *Proverb*
appeared in Buenos Aires considerably enlarged, recast, and
with a new title, *The Sphere*.[2] The author further revised the
work for its English translation which appeared in 1949 and
1950 in American and British editions respectively, identical except for the elimination in the British edition of fanciful sources
given for the philosophical passages preceding each chapter.
For the definitive Spanish version Sender followed the English
edition but made frequent revisions, adding a bit here, omitting
something there, sometimes altering the order of the text, occasionally rewriting a sentence or two, reducing the number of
chapters from sixteen to fifteen, etc.[3] In philosophical viewpoint,
however, the definitive edition remains substantially the same
as that expressed in *Proverb of Death* and its successors, *The
Sphere* of 1947, 1949, and 1950. Quotations in this chapter
from *The Sphere* are from the 1969 edition, and page numbers
in parentheses refer to it. The English translations from it as
well as from other sources in this chapter are my own.

With rare exception, in both the Spanish and English-speaking
worlds, critical reaction to *The Sphere* in its different editions
has been negative and confused. Thus far, the work has been
taken more seriously, and consequently been more appreciated,
by critics writing in the English language than by those writing
in Spanish. Juan Luis Alborg, the first Spaniard in the post-Civil
War period to devote considerable critical attention to Sender

in his two-volume study, *Hora actual de la novela española* (*The Present State of the Spanish Novel*), 1962, fails to understand the basic message of *The Sphere* and sums it up as "an abstruse allegory in which are mixed a reduced portion of approximately real human beings with a much larger quantity of symbolic, fantastic or visionary personages, in a confused mess."[4] José R. Marra-López devotes sixty-five pages to an appreciative and discerning evaluation of much of Sender's fiction, yet dismisses *The Sphere* as being unreadable, "a negative expression of a way of floating in the void by a writer removed from his roots."[5] Josefa Rivas, a Spaniard resident in the United States and author of a doctoral thesis on Sender at the University of Valencia in 1964, which she published as the first book devoted exclusively to Sender, ignored even the existence of *The Sphere*. The generally negative evaluation of the work by critics in Spain no doubt led Sender to write in a brief foreword to the 1969 edition: "Some Spanish critics have made commentaries and judgments that I respect, but which perhaps miss the central idea that I had in writing the book" (7). Rather representative of the generally unenthusiastic reception accorded the English translation of the work by North American critics are the comments by Hilda Osterhout, the novelist, who called the novel "an obscure symbolic work embodying a staggering profusion of ideas, more suited to presentation in a scientific treatise than in a novel.... 'The Sphere' is one of those freaks or experimental failures that sometimes occur in the course of a writer's development when he forgets all the techniques of his craft for the sake of a fixation or idea."[6]

On the other hand, in both the Spanish and English worlds one can find those who express admiration for *The Sphere*. Writing in 1940, David Lord declared that the book, then in its first version (*Proverb of Death*), "can hardly escape becoming a milestone in world literature."[7] In 1971 Julian Palley declared that the diverse perspectives of *The Sphere* and its "wide-ranging speculation have perplexed some critics, but for others, including the present writer, the difficulties and ambiguities—and the clarities—of *The Sphere* have served to heighten interest and admiration."[8] Marcelino C. Peñuelas, a Spaniard, devotes an appreciative chapter to the work in his excellent book, *La obra narrativa de*

Ramón J. Sender (The Narrative Work of Ramón J. Sender).[9] In his earlier book, *Conversaciones con Ramón J. Sender (Conversations with Ramón J. Sender)* Peñuelas wrote: "[*The Sphere*] is a book that to me seems clear and which disorients many readers and critics."[10] Manuel Béjar's doctoral thesis includes an intelligent exposition of the view of man found in *The Sphere*.[11]

There are, of course, two aspects to a criticism of *The Sphere,* and a literary critic must consider both of them—first, the substance or ideological content of the novel and, second, whether or not such content has been adequately fused with novelistic elements to produce an artistic unity. Most critics insist that the narrative framework of *The Sphere* is an inadequate vehicle for its heavy metaphysical and symbolical dimensions. Sherman H. Eoff who devotes ten pages of his book, *The Modern Spanish Novel,* to a penetrating and concise analysis of *The Sphere,* regards the work as "an earnest expression of contemporary man's effort to adjust to an ancient monistic view of the universe by reinterpreting it."[12] Though Eoff sees very little originality in the novel's philosophical "message," he finds that the book does contain "in incidental position, certain suggestively constructive ideas."[13] As a work of art he finds it deficient. "From the viewpoint of artistic composition," he writes, "the novelist has overstepped his license to abstain from strict rational demonstration, and the reader consequently feels that the general impression of bewilderment has been allowed to get out of hand. Apparently partaking of ideas from many quarters, the author fails to reduce them to a firm consistency."[14]

Any critical evaluation of *The Sphere,* such as that of this chapter, runs a double risk: On the one hand it becomes easy to analyze the work too closely as though it were a philosophical treatise, forgetting, in other words, that it is a novel, not an essay, and that the author must be given an artist's license to leave loose ends and unresolved problems; on the other hand, though the author must be allowed freedom as a literary artist, we have a right to expect of him a substantial and intelligible "message," more, in other words, than the mere playing with words and concepts. We demand that he fuse content and form into a coherent artistic unity. From the first Sender obviously felt that the book's content was of vital significance; in the Prologue to its first edition he wrote that he was offering his readers "the secret mechanism of giving myself"; that he had discovered immortality (an immortality that "is neither a product of differentiation nor of individualization"), and that he wished to tell others about his discovery so that his "faith might serve as a reactive leading them to the same notions."[15] Thirty years later he still believed in the basic importance of the book's message and wished for it to be understood, although he counsels the readers in a brief foreword to the definitive edition that the novel's purpose "is more illuminative than constructive, and attempts to suggest mystical planes on which the reader may build his own structures."[16] My purpose in this chapter is to evaluate the work as both art (poetry—in the broadest sense) and philosophy—and, I must add, as religion, for Sender's concepts go beyond moral and metaphysical philosophy to involve a theory of God, of Ultimate or Absolute Reality. The "mystical planes" which the work tries to suggest, as Sender says, are both poetic and religious; to him poetry and religion, in the ultimate analysis, are one and the same. Having rejected the theology of the Catholic Church and of any other institutionalized form of religion, Don Ramón creates, on the basis of his intuition and vast reading from the most disparate of sources, his own private religion or way of "personal salvation." "Although he rejected the superstitions of the others," writes the author of Saila, his alter ego, "he invented other new ones for his personal use" (141). Julia Uceda states: "Sender is, in my opinion, the only living Spanish novelist whose work has a religious dimension and sense. From the elemental human his work is a *trabajo* that seeks the metaphysical essential in an integration towards ultimate dimensions."[17]

In this chapter I shall examine Sender's world view from five different angles, all interrelated aspects of a total view of man and his place in the universe: A Spherical Universe, "Man" and "Person," The Abolition of Death, Ganglionic Wisdom, and The Morality of the "Man." The chapter will close with a brief summarizing critique of the work. Before proceeding, however, it is necessary to present, for those who have not read the novel, the main outline of its external action.

I   *The Plot of* The Sphere

As the story opens, Saila, the protagonist, a Spanish Loyalist who had just escaped to France at the conclusion of the Spanish Civil War, is leaving Paris on a train bound for Le Havre. In Le Havre he boards the transatlantic liner, the "Viscount Gall," bound for the United States. Disillusioned by the outcome of the Spanish Civil War and feeling that his true self is still back in Spain, Saila contemplates committing suicide en route. Before ending his conscious existence, however, he proposes to plumb the depths of his being in an effort to find out whether his "will to suicide" originates from his superficial "person" or from the depths of his unconscious or instinctive nature, which he poetically localizes in his most elemental nervous system, his ganglia, and which become synonymous in the novel with not only the unconscious but with essential reality, the infinite subterranean reaches of life or the "abyss" from which the great mystics have drawn their substance. It is precisely the "ganglionic world" which Saila proposes to explore before going to a watery grave, and we are led into a world of semireality and semifantasy in which almost all characters and events have both realistic and symbolic meanings. The crew and the passengers of the "Viscount Gall" become a cross section of Western humanity, although the novel primarily constitutes not so much a sociopolitical criticism as a novelized record of Sender's mystical probings, through Saila, of the ultimate nature of reality. Although the external action follows a chronological development, carefully preserved by the author, Saila's musings on the mysteries of existence follow only psychological time and are presented through various devices: italicized passages preceding each chapter, interior monologues, flashbacks in Saila's memory to former events, an inner voice, letters, dialogues and conversations, a speech by Saila, etc.

On shipboard Saila alternates his gloomy meditations with encounters with an odd assortment of human beings: Mr. Jacob Lanz (also known as Hornytoad) and his wife Christel (also known as Hilde); Mr. Cash and Carry; an American young man named Tell; Eve, a Jewess; a scientist named Mr. What; Professor However; Mrs. Sullivan; a Catholic priest; Miss Brigantine

(so called because she suggested something "afloat and pirati-
cal"); an effeminate Frenchman called Mirliflor; a bearded old
man; a Bible-quoting little old lady; a bearded stoker called the
Jebusite; and others. The last-named person, the Jebusite, is a
weird, prophetic-looking figure who rises from the bowels of
the "Viscount Gall" to proclaim that he has received a special
revelation from "Him," a mystical "Him" who cannot be described
because He "is hidden in his own light" (71). The supernatural
message transmitted by the Jebusite is that the "Viscount Gall"
should continue sailing until it encounters in the near future "a
white ship with three masts and sails spread, white keel and
masts, surrounded by white birds, beneath a sky and a sea also
white. Then . . ." (71-72). Thus the revelation is cut short. A
few days later, when a vessel meeting the stoker's description is
met on the high seas, the strange stoker leads the crew in a
mutiny. Impulsively a majority of the passengers join the crew
in proclaiming him a prophet and their leader. Under the Jebusite's mad direction the ship's officers are imprisoned, the food
supply jettisoned, and the propeller shaft sawed in two. Chaos
reigns as the ocean liner with its human cargo becomes totally
abandoned to chance. "No one is leading us," joyfully proclaims
the Jebusite. "We are totally abandoned to chance, and we no
longer sail on the 'Viscount Gall' but on a nameless ship through
an unknown space" (167). Confusion reigns among most of the
passengers, but Saila, an intuitive man who has an esoteric
understanding of the stoker, remains completely calm. Before,
during, and after this decisive event Saila frequently interrupts
his musings to have interesting encounters with fellow passengers,
including Eve, with whom he enjoys repeated sexual relations.

One day he provokes Hornytoad, a sinister character who symbolizes Hitler's intervention in the Spanish Civil War, and in
the resulting dispute Saila is forced, in self-defense, to kill him.
When brought before a jury of fellow passengers, Saila, interested only in a philosophical perspective on his deed, eloquently
defends himself, insisting that, in the final analysis, his "crime"
was merely "a bloody accident set in the perfection of God's
reality" (246). The jury, however, interested only in established
legal norms, sentences him to death. In killing Hornytoad, Saila's
suicidal obsession was transferred to the body of his victim, thus

freeing Saila. Before his execution can be effected, the "Viscount Gall" is wrecked on a sandbar. The survivors, including Saila, huddle on the unknown shore as a seaman, in a horrible scene, slowly strangles the Jebusite to death. Saila, taking Christel (Hornytoad's widow) by the hand, walks inland in a northerly direction, not knowing why. Behind them follows a group of survivors, the same group which approached Saila in a threatening manner a few minutes earlier. Thus the novel, in typically Senderian fashion, ends on an inconclusive and ambivalent note.

II   A Spherical Universe

Sender's philosophical perspective, his persistent effort to see life calmly and to see it whole, is seen in the very title of the book, *The Sphere*, a metaphor of the author's monistic conception of total reality. At bottom, he believes, all reality is one and perfect. Perhaps in all ages a sphere, drawn as perfectly as possible, has been one way of symbolizing perfection or completion, eternity, Deity. Sender once told me that he was inspired to his "spherical" theories by his reading of Aben Tofail, a Jewish mystic of the Middle Ages; Avicenna, the Persian Islamic philosopher of the eleventh century; and Ramón Lull, the Catalonian Christian philosopher and mystic of the thirteenth and fourteenth centuries.

Saila (in this case we can confidently say Sender also) was impressed with the spherical nature of the universe. Nature, he observed, is composed of an infinite number of spheres or—to be more scientifically accurate—spheroids. This is true in the finitely small—atoms, and in the infinitely large—planets, suns, the entire universe. Saila feels himself "trapped" in a space-sphere, a spheroid of water around him as well as a spheroid of the heavens above him. Likewise he is a prisoner of the time-sphere, the present. Poetically he elaborates upon the "eternal present," asking himself whether there is a future, and answering his own question.

No. There was only the present. There is nothing other than the present. Everything is present in the universe. There is nothing more living than the present. Everything fulfills itself in itself, going to another part within that present in which we are all confined. But

the present can only be conceived as an immense precinct in which
all the paths are curved, the same as on the planet and in space.
They are curved and they return to their point of origin, and it is
for that reason that all things and beings borne by their thirst to
transcend return inevitably to their origins after having passed through
their respective negations. (25–26)

"And," adds Sender to the above meditations of his literary
alter ego, "what vast distances between the yes and the no!" (26).
(The passage above is a fair sample of the poetic prose of *The
Sphere*; its prose is not ordinary prose, the writers and speakers
of which attempt to use words with reasonably precise significa-
tion, but is typical of the evocative verbalism of poetry.)

By analogy with observable physical phenomena, Saila reasons
that everything, mental and moral life included, must ultimately
be "spherical," that is all-of-a-piece, one. "Apparent" opposites,
such as light and darkness, sound and silence, love and hate,
good and evil, even life and death, are "really" one and the same
thing, spherical unities. Darkness is the "other side" of the
"light-dark" sphere, death the invisible hemisphere of the "life-
death" sphere, etc.

He felt himself acting, living, loving (conditioned by hate) or hating
(conditioned by love) spherically. The sphere of being-existing [*ser-
existir*] or of being-not being [*ser-no ser*] made difficult for him,
nevertheless, the small practical life, the little and limited movement
that links him with others, and makes up the surface reality of a
normal life, but on the other hand in each of those spheres he had
a sensation of totality, a "transcending in the ineffable," . . . For Saila,
the sphere was the final "what." (69, emphasis added)

A preoccupation with the reconciliation of apparent opposites
such as life and death, love and hate, into higher unities or
syntheses here called "spheres," has been a constant in Sender's
literary production. A conception of ultimate reality as monistic—
and pantheistic, also—is seen in the following quotation from
Pro Patria, Sender's first novel, in which Viance, hiding from the
enemy in the belly of a dead horse on the Moroccan battlefield,
suddenly understands "that his own matter is alike to that which
encircles him, that *there is only one kind of matter*, and that all

of it is animated by the same blind impulses, obedient to the same law. A vague tenderness mounts in him, a longing to do what is good and to find everything sweet and kind" (emphasis added).[18] But Don Ramón's interest in the fusion of apparent opposites is not just a literary concern or pose. Although he always evinces a doubting or skeptical attitude toward even his most cherished speculations, Sender sees the sphere as symbolic of the final "what" of things. In an address in 1949 to the Phi Kappa Phi chapter of the University of New Mexico, Sender stated: "[The notion] . . . that life and death are not contradictory . . . is necessary in order to oppose to the growing danger not only a growing essential serenity, but also a new essentiality. Let us try to make the determinant norm of our life crystallize in that place in our consciousness *where life and death are terms of the same equation.* Out of that equation will come the new form of heroism, that is to say, the new form of essential action, which humanity is waiting for" (emphasis added).[19] The essence of the "spherical" theory is its resolution of "apparent" dualities into "real" unities, two terms, as it were, "of the same equation."

An important facet of Sender's "spherical" theories is his peculiar antithesis, "man" and "person," to which we shall now turn our attention.

III   *"Man" and "Person"*

In *The Sphere* man is viewed as a dichotomy: "man" and "person." "Man and person are antipodal," Sender writes in the passage preceding Chapter V. "Man is fact. Pure fact. Person is reflection, the recoiling of fact back upon itself" (97). "Man" is fact; the "person" merely a reflection or recoil upon itself. "Man" or "manhood" (*hombría*) is man's essence, his roots in eternity. "The ganglia are the nucleus of manhood" (97). Man "is the source of all truth, of each universal and innate truth" (97). The "person" is man's mask, the individualization of his personality which begins at birth, or soon thereafter, and grows throughout life; loosely speaking, it is man's self-consciousness. The basic question posed by Sender in *The Sphere*, according to Sherman Eoff is: "Does one's self-consciousness have meaning as a separate reflective entity, or is it significant only as identified with a vast undying and unthinking 'world spirit'?"[20]

The "person" is temporal, the product of experience in this life, that which differentiates and isolates one man from another, while the "man" is eternal, undifferentiated "manhood." For the "man" death cannot exist; the "person," on the other hand, fears its death, its extinction and reabsorption into the undifferentiated essence of the species.

Sender has, in effect, deified what he refers to as *el hombre* ("man") or *hombría* ("manhood" or "man-ness"), a mystical essence which gives every man his true worth. Although all men by virtue of being men partake of *hombría* passively and unconsciously, there seems to be room in Sender's thought for individual man to cooperate actively and in a twilight zone between consciousness and unconsciousness in the formation of an "essential self," a "self" which is both individuated in the human being and yet integral with pure, liberated *hombría* at a mystical level; in death this "essential self" joyfully returns to its source, the Great All or the Great Nothing. The *individuated* "essential self" must be distinguished from the *individualization* or personalization of the *persona*, as Manuel Béjar points out.[21] So in a sense one can conceive of the indivdual's "essential self" as being linked intimately with pure essence, yet assuming a limited "self" expression because of the individuation (not individualization) of the human being, a kind of intermediate "self" between the "person" and the universal "man." Some men cultivate the "man" assiduously and thus develop strong "essential selves"; others ignore their true human essence and become almost totally persons or masks; men, in Sender's terminology, without "substance." There is an affinity but no consistent parallel between Sender's dichotomy and the modern Existentialist distinction between the *authentic* self and the unauthentic self.

Obviously Sender's view of man differs sharply from that held by Miguel de Unamuno. While Don Miguel emphasized the value of the individual person not merely because he is *human*, but also because he is *individual*, Sender finds man's ultimate worth only in his humanness, in the species. Sender's "man"—abstract, absolute, mystical essence—would be in Unamunoesque terms, a "no-man." For the Salamancan thinker, survival must be completely individual, of Miguel de Unamuno, no less; for Don Ramón life after death will not be a continuation of Ramón

José Sender but only of his universal "manhood." Man's real value is not in his individual personality, his "person," but only in his inner essence, his "essential self" (insofar as "self" here expresses some kind of individuation of "essence," a kind of imprisonment within the human being while he lives), in which he is part and parcel of a larger whole—"Man"—God Himself. As seen in Chapter 4, Sabino, in *A Man's Place*, was valuable because he was part of "Man," not because he was an *individual* human being. Sender's humanism—his religion—is, therefore, collectivist and Pantheistic. As such it contrasts directly with traditional Christianity which maintains that God is transcendent, utterly distinct and apart from all his creation, including His supreme handiwork, man. To Sender man is an integral part of God; "God" is the incomprehensible totality while "man" is a somewhat more limited concept, just as in Christian theology Jesus is God yet there is a distinction between God and Jesus.

Rafael Pérez Sandoval, who has studied Don Ramón's religious beliefs, writes:

Sender's reverence toward God is shown in his reverence toward man. He believes, as does Spinoza, that man is an integral part of *the infinite intellect of God*. That is why, according to Sender, man's religious activity is directly related to his essential actions since man is part of the cosmic process in the constant fight against nothingness. In Sender's opinion, man guides himself by the blind tendency of his instincts toward truth, love, justice, beauty, and perfection.

The absolute and only reality for Sender is God expressing Himself and being, Himself, a part of His creation. He is always hidden behind the mysteries that surround us. Thus, Sender observes that the mysteries are not only in the macrocosm, or in the outside world, but also in the microcosm of our emotions, sensory perceptions and intellect.[22]

Since man is "an integral part of *the infinite intellect of God*," any offense to the human species, even to an individual member of that species, becomes essentially an offense to God Himself. Thus, Sender's reverence toward God, as Pérez Sandoval states, "is shown in his reverence toward man." This exaltation of man for the simple fact that he is human is a constant in all of Sender's work; its mystical dimension is perhaps most successfully novel-

ized in *A Man's Place*. A hero of one of the author's short stories
on Mexican life, Navalatl, expresses the Senderian humanism:
"The only interests are those of man. And man is the fire that was
neither born nor will be extinguished."[23]

A principal theme of the great novelist, Pío Baroja, was *la
lucha por la vida* (the struggle for life); a theme running through
all Senderian works might be termed *the struggle for human
dignity*—"dignity" here being used to mean the intrinsic worth
of the human being, his *hombría*. Viance in *Pro Patria*, the
Journalist in *Public Order*, Evaristo the Frogman in *The Night
of One Hundred Heads*, Sabino in *A Man's Place*, Pepe in the
monumental three-volume autobiographical series, *Chronicle of
Dawn*, Saila in *The Sphere*, Rómulo in *El rey y la reina* (*The
King and the Queen*), and others—all sought to live on the
deeper level of their own "manhood," that mystical essence which
Sender believes to be divine, and which, therefore, endues man
with lasting worth.

On board the "Viscount Gall" there is a clash between Saila,
a follower of "manhood" (who hardly has a "person") and the
representatives of the superficial "person," for example, Mr. What
and Professor However—who hate Salia—(158), Hornytoad, Miss
Brigantine, Tell the American, and others. After the encounter
with the white ship and the abandonment of the "Viscount
Gall" to chance (symbolic of a descent to the essential level
of life—the level of "man"), Saila and Eve (symbol of the natural
woman) along with the mad Jebusite find themselves in their
true element while the others are bewildered.

In respect for people simply because they are human, Sender
differs little, if any, from other great writers. In his emphasis
upon a sense of corporate man he is in line with the trend of
current world literature. His humanism is perhaps most distinctive in its radical reaction against the excessive individualization of people in Western European industrialized cultures
in this century especially, an individualization that has isolated
the individual and led to a growing depersonalization of life.
Sender's attitude is seen in Saila's rejection of the "person" in
favor of that part of him which is one with all other men—at
the deep level of the mystically corporate man. A new morality,
collectivist or corporate in nature rather than individualistic, and

which I shall discuss later, can be built upon Sender's theory of "man" and "person." The need for human solidarity which Sender saw in the forties is no less urgent in subsequent decades if civilization is to survive. But I am here getting ahead of myself. Let us now turn our attention to perhaps the central thesis of *The Sphere*, the notion that death—for the "man"—does not exist.

IV *The Abolition of Death*

"Whether consciously or not," Salvador de Madariaga writes, "the Spaniard lives against a background of eternity, and his outlook is more religious than philosophic."[24] Sender's whole novelistic production has been written "against a background of eternity": death has been a constant preoccupation, almost an obsession, with Don Ramón. He has dealt with the subject of death more extensively, more profoundly, and more artistically than have any of his Spanish contemporaries; perhaps second place in the treatment of the theme should go to José Luis Castillo Puche, author of the excellent novel, *Con la muerte al hombro* (*With Death at Your Shoulder*), 1954.

Sender deals rather extensively with death in *The Word Became Sex (Theresa of Jesus)*, a novel briefly discussed in Chapter 3. I quote from the novel—written, according to Sender, when he was fifteen or sixteen years old—here to demonstrate the author's early fascination with the mystery of death. While on a journey Saint Theresa pondered: "What's that about dying or living? They say that the dead neither move nor speak. But one can hardly know what dead people think? And, nevertheless, they are the ones who think most intensely. The pupils, upon losing their outward view, turn around and look at grand interior panoramas with a passionate or humorous vision."[25] How much like the Sender of *The Sphere* do these lines sound! The unity in fundamental substance and vision that Sender's narratives across four decades have shown is noteworthy. Exploring a few fundamental ideas or notions, he has novelized them from widely different angles and under a vast variety of conditions, times, places, and situations. Many great writers have done the same.

The fundamental thesis of *The Sphere*, that death does not

exist, is based directly on the "man-person" dichotomy that I have already examined. Death is the person, that growing individualization of the human being which differentiates and isolates him from all other men, which takes him farther and farther away from his eternal substance, the subterranean man. Comments Eoff: "Unwilling to accept the idea that death is a substantial aspect of reality, the author Sender seeks to identify himself with generic manhood (*hombría*), which he proclaims a partner with God in God's eternal struggle against nothingness. He thus tries to avoid what he calls 'the error of Kierkegaard and perhaps of Christianity,' the error of presupposing 'an independent person—differentiated enough to imagine itself free—that can do nothing with its freedom.'"[26]

For Unamuno, who proclaimed that "the supreme human need is the need of not dying, the need of enjoying for ever the plenitude of our own individual limitation," survival after death must be of Miguel de Unamuno. The survival of the mystical "essential self" reabsorbed into mystical essentiality is the only possibility that Sender's tentative views leave open; it would not satisfy Unamuno.

In 1952 Sender told me: "I am not interested that Ramón Sender should continue living beyond death. That would be an absurdity. The person, that is to say, the individual, will die. What survives is man or *hombría*. The person is the product of experience. Person is reason, that part of us that increases with age. It is precisely this individualization of the human being that dies. We see this phenomenon repeated in nature every day; for example, the coming and going of individual clouds [the clouds perish but *clouds* continue, that is to say, they are "eternal"]."[27] "Man," therefore, I repeat, is eternal; the "person" is temporal. Death can be conceived as a great sea or reservoir from which we rise at birth, go through our life cycle, and return at death. "In a newborn child all mystery is to be found," writes Sender. "In a being brought—condemned, if one prefers—to the temporality of living, and saved at last from that temporality."[28] The source and the end of man, therefore, is "man"—absolute man.

An individual's death would be imperfectly analogous to a river with the ocean. And just as water from the ocean through natural phenomena finds its way back to streams and rivers, so absolute "man" "gives birth" to individual man who lives and eventually dies, i.e., returns to his source, undying "man," or "Man."

While in the ship's prison for having killed Hornytoad, Saila writes long letters to Eve, consisting of poetic-philosophical musings generally expressive of Sender's special outlook toward life and death. Some of these poetic statements are esoteric, but those that I quote below are intelligible—at least within the framework of a "spherical" outlook.

I am something like a tree that speaks, but life has let me only stammer. (262)

How small my hands for all that life has wanted to give me! (264)

I am a true eagle, but one with vertigo. (264)

Everything destroys itself, affirming itself. (264)

We come from life and we go back to life. Life itself comes from life and returns to itself. This would be tiring and would overwhelm us were we not able to create for ourselves, with death, the illusion of a concrete dimension. (265)

I have an intermittent wisdom: the dream. (265)

In Sender's *Las criaturas saturnianas* (*The Saturnine Creatures*), 1968, the protagonist, Princess Tarakanova, at age twenty-nine, thought "that the most important task of the life of each of us is his death. The destruction of one in which God collaborates in an important and effective way. The slow task—at times rapid—of the destruction of each one of us. That was the only thing that mattered in every case."[29] The affirmative attitude expressed here as well as in *The Sphere* toward "one's destruction" is understandable only in the light of what I have been discussing in this chapter: in the eternal, universal essence all is perfect, all is positive, Absolute Reality, God. To die, then, is really to allow God, Absolute Reality, to erase the imperfections of the relative person, to rectify, as it were, a mistake—the individualized "person" who can be compared to a tumor springing up on the surface of reality. Sender's assumption is that in ultimate reality all things and qualities are one and perfect.

That which here is "apparently" a duality is there "really" a
unity. Ultimately everything is perfect, good, as can be deduced
from the following: "Man [essential reality] lacks possibilities
of negation. That which negates is the person. Man only feels
life and he feels himself . . . in an affirmative manner. He is absolute in his affirmations, and the negations of the person are
nothing but the conditions of affirmation" (138).

Death is the person; life the man, I repeat. The fear of death
is all but universal, yet there have been those who through a
sense of the totality of reality, a totality which comprehends
both "life" and "death," obtained through revelation or reasoning
or both, have eagerly welcomed death. The Apostle Paul was
one such, for he writes that for him "to live is Christ, and to die
is gain. If it is to be life in the flesh, that means fruitful labor
for me. Yet which I shall choose I cannot tell. I am hard pressed
between the two. My desire is to depart and be with Christ, for
that is far better. But to remain in the flesh is more necessary
on your account."[30] But Paul and Sender are poles apart: Paul
believed firmly in the continuance and supreme contentment of
his individual self-consciousness after his physical disintegration;
Sender's position allows only for the self (consciousness) to pass
along the continuum of the eternal present (in which we are
all confined) to be absorbed in the Great All, i.e., to become a
"non-self," no longer to realize one's personal reality or to have
consciousness as an individual. Whereas Paul's God is a personal
and knowable God (even though not exhaustively knowable),
Sender's is undefinable, a vague abstraction which may be All
or may be Nothing.

V   *Ganglionic Wisdom*

On the open deck of the "Viscount Gall" Saila broods and
meditates on death—the unknown. As I said earlier, he wishes
to ascertain whether his "will to suicide" originates from his
reason or from the depths of his instinctive or unconscious nature, which he verbally localizes in his ganglia. The relationship
between *hombría*, discussed earlier, and his ganglia he expresses
as follows: "The ganglia are the nucleus of manhood" (97). In
Senderian terminology the following terms are used loosely as

synonyms of the ganglia: "the subterranean reaches of life";[31] "the abyss";[32] the "primordial, simple and primitive";[33] the dream; essential reality; the unconscious or, as Sender usually prefers to call it, the subconscious; absolute reality; the ineffable (*lo inefable*); "real reality"; "the primitive and elementary human."[34] Sender was probaly influenced in his theory of the ganglia by his reading of Schopenhauer. Eoff points out that more than a century before the appearance of *The Sphere*, Schopenhauer "had declared that 'the ganglion system, i.e., the subjective nervous system,' which in the lower forms of life is predominant over the objective or cerebral system, was merely the physiological process by which instinct, while serving the species, performed an illusionistic role as regards the individual."[35]

Saila cultivates contact with his ganglia by relaxation, by momentarily breaking free from the tyranny of reason (or at least creating the illusion of such a break) to feel a mystical or intuitive unity with all created life—animal, plant, and mineral life as well as human—(an experiencing of what might be called the "unity of all created beings" which seems to parallel the experience of nature mystics). "Only when we listen," Sender once told me, "do we become aware of the inner voices. We discover voices in our ganglia."[36] Again, it should be emphasized, Sender takes very seriously his "ganglionic theory"; he is not playing mere word games. He is a literary mystic; to his last statement above he added, "There is in this a bit of mysticism." Don Ramón, strictly a twentieth-century writer, has lost faith in the strictly rational; in a kind of frustrated rage against the closed (and impersonal) circle of a naturalistic explanation for all phenomena he has sought to emphasize man's unconscious and to endow it with a kind of mysterious "personality." To him the ganglia represent a scarcely tapped infinite reservoir of potential knowledge, of unassimilated truth, of poetic inspiration, heroism, and holiness.

The dramatic tension of *The Sphere*, as it is in all of Sender's fiction, is, therefore, between two worlds: the one of relative appearances, of the conscious, conventional, rationalistic, unauthentic person imprisoned by the physical world and a positivist turn of mind *versus* the world of divine disorder, the unconscious and absolute world of dreams, of the passionate and natural (or authentic) man. Sender seeks ever to write in the twilight zone where these two "worlds" or "hemispheres" merge —where, as Baudelaire put it, he can observe the *matérialisation du miracle*.

Saila is in search of his roots, his ganglia, and in his search he has largely dissociated himself from the superficial, everyday reality of the "person," becoming, in his "ganglionic" stupor, socially maladjusted on shipboard. Contemplating suicide, he reflects to himself: ". . . I hardly have a person. I am all ganglia, and therefore my death will be a minimal death when it comes" (91).

Perhaps I may momentarily digress here to ask a question which is not altogether impertinent: Was Saila merely suffering from war psychosis? Were he a real person, he could be examined for evidence of pathology, but all that we know of him is what Sender wrote. Yet we may ask: Has Sender portrayed a psychotic in spite of himself, i.e., Saila considered from a clinical standpoint as one thing which from a literary viewpoint might be called something else? A medical doctor defined psychoses as "forms of mental disease in which the person becomes separated from reality and is living in another world. He may see objects and hear voices that are not actually there, or he may have ideas that he is someone other than himself. Many of these patients have difficulty in memory and in associating things, so that their thoughts are disorganized and without reason."

Saila certainly exhibits symptoms of psychosis: dissociation from reality, seeing objects that are not there (he sees a dog with a man's face), hearing voices that are not there (he hears a man's voice coming from a dog), a feeling of self-estrangement, disorganized mental processes, a faulty memory. Reading the following passages (in a clinical casebook, for example), a psychiatrist might diagnose Saila as a psychotic:

. . . that which [to Saila] seemed most naturally his, the phenomena of his soul, the mechanics of memory and all sentiments, he perceived outside of himself. That is to say, he was able to "objectify" them. Estranged. (13)

He [Saila] did not know where his luggage was. . . . Why all this difficulty in remembering, especially recent things? (16–17)

Saila felt happy, and he tried to benefit from that disposition by "thinking with reason," with that reason of which he was so tired. But he couldn't. "I should like to think with my elbow, with my ankles." At times he thought that it was from them that he had confused but powerful suggestions that controlled his remaining stimuli. (46)

Perhaps, from a clinical standpoint, Saila can be regarded as a psychotic. So what? If he is "insane," his "insanity" is akin to that of Don Quixote or Saint Theresa. We are not interested in Don Quixote when at the end of his life he had recovered his "sanity," but only in him in his quixotic state. In 1968 Sender told me in a conversation that all people fall into two categories: *los locos y los tontos* ("madmen and fools"). In the final edition of *The Sphere* Sender has introduced this idea, missing in former editions: "What is bad about humanity—Saila repeated to himself—is that some conduct themselves stupidly and others outrageously and incongruously. Some madmen and others fools" (170). The *locos* or "madmen" are the "natural" men as contrasted with the "social, artificial" men; they are the "ganglionic" men and not the restricted men of reason (Mr. What and Professor However); the men of *hombría* and not the men of the *persona*. Saila, of course, was a *loco* in this sense, but there was one man on board who had been even more overcome by the "dazzlement" caused by contact with the chaotic world of the ganglia than had Saila; that man was the weird stoker, the Jebusite. "Saila saw in the Jebusite a man without a person, with even less person than he himself had" (181). It is necessary to oppose reason to the ganglia to preserve the harmonious unity of the senses, to avoid, in other words, becoming "lost." Thinking of the Jebusite, Saila saw in him "a type all ganglia" (72). And it is precisely the "madness" of the Jebusite that Saila finds fascinating: "Although he is crazy, really crazy," muses Saila, "one may and one must talk with him. When a madman makes himself understood, and especially when he convinces us of something—it makes no difference about what—how he does convince us and enrich us!" (76–77). Although Salia believes himself to be in "absolute reality" (258), listening to whispering voices "on the level where virgin notions are formed" (185), he has not yet succumbed to the "blindness through the dazzlement" as have madmen (69). Nevertheless, he feels the danger, for he writes to Eve: "I have seen so much that at times I think that out of vengeance mystery is going to swallow me up" (275). *Locos,* such as the Jebusite, have been swallowed up by mystery, the chaotic underground world of primeval substance, of a strange and unknowable divinity.

On almost every page of the novel one finds what might be termed a "reversal of values." The unconscious is preferred over the conscious; intuition over reason; the ganglia over the brain; abstract "man" over the concrete, individual person; death over life; potential knowledge over actual knowledge; dream over apparent reality; eternity over temporality; mystery over clarity; a state of anarchy over a state of law and order, etc. The relative devaluation of the apparent, everyday world of order and logic in which we usually live is a necessary corollary of the book's passionate exaltation of the unconscious or underlying world of disorder, dreams, and irrational forces. Indeed, the true adventure of *The Sphere* can only be understood as Saila's exploration of the underworld, his plunge to the bottom of the unknown, the unconscious, the abyss, the ganglionic world, in order to decipher the mysteries of life. The book opens with a speculative passage which makes this purpose clear; we have minds "not in order to understand but especially in order 'not to understand too much.' What horrible or ineffable truths come to our intelligence, and 'remain outside'? Against what revelations or evidences intelligence defends us?" (9). Saila argues "That all things in life were ruled by magic and mystery" (176).

A constant in Sender's total work, and a key to his *Weltanschauung,* is his belief in the almost all-powerful role of the unconscious, both individual and collective, in determining man's fate. Freud and Jung, as I indicated in Chapter 2, have left their mark on all contemporary literary artists, including Don Ramón. Yet one must insist that though modern psychology converges here with the powerful mystical vein in the Spanish literary and artistic heritage, *Sender owes more to Saint Theresa than he does to Freud or Jung.*[37] The author's deep and sustained interest in the Avilese saint, the general nature and direction of his interest in mystery, as well as his thoroughly Spanish vision of life support my view.

For Sender the task of literary creation is first a "discovery" of new truth in the "abyss," the realm of the ganglia. Saila's lonely probing of his deepest essence parallels this first step, a "search" more passive than active in nature. In an article in *View*, a Neo-Surrealist magazine, Sender explains that a whole philosophy can be involved in the mechanics of discovering poetic truth. Stating that "modern physics shows that our eyes see only sixteen per cent of the things whose existence can be proved by other means," he deduces that not only our eyes, but our ears and other "forms of sensitivity are of much more use to us as defenses than as perceptive and assimilative elements. . . . I am convinced that our reason serves not only as a means to understand, but above all as a way to keep from understanding too much."[38] We may open ourselves to "the permanent campaign of ideas attacking us from all sides, trying at all costs to penetrate into our interior" through weakening our resistances, the weakest, and therefore most appropriate, of which is the imagination. This weakening of our resistances, he goes on to say, "can be called disintegration," a phenomenon experienced by many painters, musicians, and poets.[39] "The entire secret of modern art," he concludes, "lies in being able to disintegrate oneself without becoming lost."[40]

Saila can be described as one whose resistances have been weakened, weakened by the trauma of Civil War and defeat as well as by his deliberate attempt to open himself to "ganglionic" truth. He has taken only the *first* step toward literary creation; more than intuition is needed for the completion of literary creation since the "discovered reality" must be translated into the relative elements of language; it must be made to *communicate* something to others, and for this final step reason must be employed. The author recognizes the place for reason in his very important essay, "On a Really Austere Aesthetic," in which he writes: "Dreams, extravagances and sensual lyrics burst forth like lights of promise from this abyss of mysteries and miracles [the unconscious]. Reason has completed the prodigy with the minimum of experience indispensable for their expression. From this it may be deduced that it is not the combination of what is already known and put in order, *but the ordering of infinite chaos*, that comprehends and glorifies all the labor of the poet and the hero and the saint."[41] For Sender, literary creation consists not in commentary or reflection upon what is already known—the task of the academies—but in the expression or "creation" of hitherto unassimilated material found in that realm of "mysteries and miracles," the unconscious—or in Saila's terminology, the ganglia. For that final step of expression there can be no substitute for talent and at least a minimum of reason, the same "reason" which is the product of the brain, "that ancient tumor of the ganglia" (190).

To be in Sender's company, as I have been on various occasions, is to be made aware of the marvel and mystery underlying, almost immersing our conscious lives. To read him is also to experience the subtle interpenetration of the visible and the invisible "worlds," and to awaken to a sense of mystery, poetic in nature, that can enrich and free the individual, though fleetingly, from his physical limits and the confines imposed upon him by a rationalistic, positivistic way of conceiving reality.

It should be clear that Sender (and, consequently, this study) does not use the term, "the unconscious," with scientific accuracy. Whereas, for example, Sender regards the unconscious as the infinite dimension of life, Freud placed the infinite outside man's unconscious. It is apparent from *The Sphere* and in the author's published statements on the subject *passim* that he regards the unconscious as the source of all the great myths of the human race, of religions, of poetry, and of heroism.[42]

"Let us love our ganglia that know more about ourselves than our reason," writes Sender. "Man knows much more than he believes he knows, and that unexpressed wisdom is in the ganglionic. There are the things that are still without name, secrets about ourselves, the great mysteries. From there the truth shouts out to us" (210). The unconscious, although localized in each individual in his ganglia, is essentially a collective, universal unconsciousness, not the individual's own unconscious, of which the psychologists talk. The frontier between the individual and the universal totality in Sender's novel becomes, of necessity, shrouded in impenetrable mystery. To seek to "clarify" the mechanics of the relation of the individual and the universal in this dark area would be to do so only in a verbal, rather than actual, sense. The purpose of the novel—I quote again from

Sender's foreword to the definitive edition—"is more illuminative than constructive, and attempts to suggest mystical planes on which the reader may build his own structures" (7). If as Ford Madox Ford once wrote, the word "author" means "someone who adds to your consciousness,"[43] then Sender is preeminently an author; indeed, his principal driving urge in writing is just that—to express "new realities." Sender says: "Yes, a poem, a novel in reality is just that: a problem between the unconscious and consciousness, that is, a dream the writer has the duty to make verisimilar."[44] Of course, Sender, like all authors, is not always successful in communicating his truth, in making his dreams "verisimilar." Rather than to submit a dream too closely to the cold (and deadening) light of reason, he prefers to leave it in that twilight zone where mystery still stirs the imagination.

VI   *The Morality of the "Man"*

A secondary theme of *The Sphere* is Saila's rejection of traditional morality. On the one hand he spurns all moral absolutes as conceived by the Judeo-Christian background of Western European culture and civilization (a prescriptive morality), and on the other hand he rejects a morality which is merely the consensus of what is for the common good at different times and places, an ethics, in other words, determined by a head-count (a descriptive morality).

Having been brought to trial by his fellow passengers on board the "Viscount Gall" for having killed Mr. Jacob Lanz (Hornytoad), Saila makes a long, abstract defense of his position from the standpoint of the "spherical" or perfect nature of ultimate reality. Morality as generally understood, he argues, is negative, "salvation through negatives: I do not kill, I rob not, I do not violate" (242). But final reality cannot be negative; it is always "active, dynamic and affirmative" (242). He affirms a "ganglionic" morality, a morality of the "man" as opposed to that of the "person." "That body of laws that you invoke is the product of a reason with which we want to be individual, personal, unique. It is in the pusillanimous soul that keeps an inhibitory morality, and which our affirmative ganglia refuse.... A morality of manhood (*hombría*) is mine" (245). "There is a moral man," argues Saila, "and a moral person. I stick to the man" (247).

But we must ask: How can Saila meaningfully talk of the "moral man"? Saila's morality of the "man" would, first of all, put the interests of the human species above the interests of any single individual; it would be collectivist rather than individualist. Here we find Sender's thoughts directly in line with scientific humanism (which stresses the collective) as well as with the doctrinaire attitude of Soviet Russia, Communist China, and even of Nazi Germany—all of which sacrificed the individual in the name of the "collective good." Obviously there is grave danger when any one man or group of men is allowed to determine what the "best" interests of the human species are. The danger increases in proportion to the political power possessed by such men. Yet, despite the impracticality of his position, Saila can be admired for his bold formulation of his own "morality"; his adherence to his "essential self" parallels the loyalty of the modern Existentialist hero to his "authentic self."

Though Saila's rebelliousness against the status quo, the sociopolitical Establishment, is apparent in *The Sphere*, Eoff correctly points out that the book's "primary viewpoint remains philosophical."[45] The principal philosophical objection to Saila's brand of "morality" is that it is a personal, subjective view of "right" and "wrong"; it is, therefore, entirely relative and like a mystical experience or a drug "trip," essentially incapable of being adequately communicated to others. A major difficulty lies in *how* we are to determine what the real interests of the species are in practical, concrete situations. Another problem is man's general inability to follow such a noble "morality." One is grimly reminded that even Hitler may have been convinced (from the peculiar perspective of his world view) of the "essential morality" of strengthening the human species through his elimination of its weaker members; he, in the current jargon, was "doing his own thing." When man rejects moral absolutes, he is left only with opinions as to what is right and what is wrong; having no absolute yardstick, morality for society can then only be determined by *what is*—current practices—and the taking of a head-count to determine what the majority desires, or by the arbitrary decision of a dictatorship.

After all his rationalizations are finished, Saila still doubts. This, of course, is typical of Sender; he always evinces a questioning, ambivalent view toward reality, never dogmatizing (despite his appearance of doing so). Throughout the novel there is the dialectic of reason versus intuition: "Reason told him no, and his ganglia yes" (90). The synthesis at which Sender arrives is always a tentative "perhaps." Saila's meditations frequently end, as does the story itself (in a symbolic sense), with a question. At the end of the novel a hostile group follows Saila and Christel as they strike inland from the shore on which the "Viscount Gall" was wrecked. Would the group demand of Saila an expiation for his "crimes" as it had of the Jebusite?

VII   Conclusion

The Sphere is an ambitious attempt to fuse into an artistic unity the realistic, the lyrical-metaphysical, the fantastic, and the symbolic. Has Sender succeeded? Only to a limited extent. The narrative framework is inadequate to carry the excessively heavy charge of poetic, philosophical, and symbolic meaning. The narrative element can move only sluggishly in its labyrinth of levels, dimensions, and meanings.

The author's primary intention seems to be to create for the reader the vivid world of Saila, Sender's own world, to put him into the center of that peculiar and strange world, to cause him to see from there reality from the perspective of Saila's ganglionic stupor, to awaken within him lyric emotion through association with the incongruent and the marvelous. In short, the novel dramatizes the clash between the world of surface realities (Mr. Cash and Carry, Mr. What, Professor However, the Catholic priest, etc.) and the underlying world of the poets and the religious prophets (Saila and the Jebusite, respectively). Continuity of time and mood are maintained, and the story is one story, the story of Saila's exploration of the unconscious and reintegration of his personality after the trauma of the Spanish Civil War; the narrative opens with the protagonist beginning a journey and closes with the end of that voyage. The climax of its tenuous "plot" is reached when Saila kills Hornytoad and in the act finds that his will to suicide has been transferred to the dead body of his victim.

There are important elements in the novel which have been only alluded to in this chapter, and which call for detailed study which space does not permit here. For example, the symbolism of the work: The title of the novel itself is symbolic of the monistic viewpoint of the protagonist; the encounter of the white ship symbolizes death, the entering of "real reality"; Eve represents the "natural woman" or Nature; Christel the "eternal woman" with her appeal to the incongruous; Mr. Cash and Carry the moneyed interests of society; the Catholic priest the Christian church; Mr. What the spirit of logic narrowly conceived, and of law and order; Professor However, the academic, noncreative, nonimaginative mind. The "Viscount Gall" becomes destiny and its human cargo the condition of man, especially Western man, in the twentieth century. Social satire is superb, generously distributed, and its humor serves to counter the excessive somberness of the novel.

Julian Palley affirms that *The Sphere* "is a successful work of art, because it creates for us a meaningful myth of man's responsibility and guilt in the twentieth century."[46] He adds: "What is undeniable is that Sender is the only Spanish novelist of our time who has dealt with the Civil War and its aftermath in the light of philosophical and existential ideas that have dominated the best modern thought and literature."[47] I agree with this last statement by Palley.

CHAPTER 6

The King and the Queen

AN allegorical yet realistic narrative, *El rey y la reina* (*The King and the Queen*) is written in poetic prose freighted with symbolic and metaphysical meaning. With its typically Senderian emphasis on purely human values, it poses the question of the ultimate nature of reality and of man's relationship to that reality, a reality conceived of especially as the realm of the absolute ideal. Possibly Sender's finest novel, *The King and the Queen,* translated into English by Mary Low, appeared in 1948, one year before the original Spanish, and evoked brief but penetrating comments from Robert B. Heilman as part of a review article published by him in the fall of 1948.[1] Yet the novel, in the twenty-five years since its initial appearance, has aroused only a modicum of critical interest.[2] The fact that its first Spanish reprint appeared in Spain as late as 1970[3]—its first open access to the general reading public there—explains in part the lack of attention from Spanish critics. Quotations from *The King and the Queen* used in this chapter are taken from the Universal Library Edition (New York: Grosset and Dunlap, 1968), and numbers in parentheses refer to pages in it. Henceforth I shall refer to the work simply as *The King.*

As fiction, *The King* is a vast improvement over *The Sphere.* In *The King,* the narrative element fuses with the book's poetic and philosophical intentions much more effectively than in *The Sphere.* On the surface the story is of a gardener's almost fanatical efforts to protect his mistress, the Duchess of Alcanadre, from Republican militiamen while she is hiding in an unused tower in her palace in Madrid during the Spanish Civil War. On a deeper level it is a sociopsychological study of conflicts in the minds of both the middle-aged Andalusian gardener, Rómulo, and the Duchess as war upsets the conventional relationships between these two members of different social classes, plebeian and noble. In the end the Duchess comes to accept Rómulo, not as a mere servitor, but as a "man." On this level the progressively changing attitudes of both the Duchess and of Rómulo constitute a commentary on the Civil War inasmuch as the exigencies of war temporarily overcome traditional class barriers; on a symbolic sociopsychological level, Rómulo represents the Spanish people (the *pueblo*) and the Duchess traditional Spain;[4] on the highest level, the story is of Rómulo's private search—in the midst of the upheavals of war—for his own *ideal reality*, a dramatization, in other words, of man's universal aspiration toward the ideal, after Dulcinea (Rómulo is Don Quixote, the Duchess is Dulcinea), and of the impossibility of total or absolute possession of that ideal.

On the morning before the outbreak of the Civil War, the beautiful Duchess, while swimming in the nude in the basement pool of her palace in Madrid, receives word that her gardener awaits outside with a message for her. As though impelled by some unconscious desire—perhaps to be known in some fuller and more passionate way than she has hitherto experienced from her life with the Duke, "an amiable, upright man with a great regard for social conventions" (7)—she flippantly orders Rómulo to come in. When the maid protests, "My Lady, it's a man," she disdainfully replies, "Rómulo a man?" (9). Accustomed to unquestioning obedience, the gardener enters and while the Duchess calmly floats naked on her back he hands her the message. Thinking that to avert his gaze would be to proclaim the impropriety of the situation, "he remained looking at her unblinkingly and also—it must be said—*unseeingly*" (9, emphasis added). The startled maid murmurs: "Things happen to the mistress like in dreams!'" (10).

Rómulo leaves with his head spinning. To him his "unseeing" vision of Her Grace's nakedness has the effect of an epiphany, a dazzling glimpse of absolute reality. The heart of the novel is the gardener's quest for the full meaning and development of his startling experience, his awakening to an ideal reality beneath the surface of life. His private quest, of course, is set against the violent background of war with its many social and political implications. With the beginning of conflict the next day, the Duke leaves to join the Nationalist forces while the Duchess, thinking that the war will last only a few days, remains in the palace hiding, with Rómulo's connivance, on the top floor of an unused five-story tower at one remote wing of the palace. That very day the Government militia commandeer the palace and its grounds, dismissing all the servants except Rómulo who, by fortunate chance, had secretly joined (against palace regulations) some months before a labor union—probably the National Labor Federation (Confederación Nacional de Trabajo). Trusting Rómulo, the militiamen make him custodian of the palace.

Although Rómulo supports the Republican cause, he resolves, *because of the swimming pool incident,* to protect the Duchess at all costs, to put Her Grace—the transcendental ideal—above all partisan interests. As the war deepens, he finds it increasingly difficult to protect her. Soon a recruiting center and an antitank training unit are established on the ducal grounds. During these hectic days Rómulo suffers many anxieties for the safety of Her Grace. The motif of nakedness—in the gardener's imagination—recurs again and again throughout the novel: "Rómulo recalled the duchess in the nude. 'It's that nakedness that's caused all this confusion,' he said to himself, quite convinced. 'How? Why? That I shall never know' " (23).

The nudity of the Duchess symbolizes hidden "realities" in life, the realm of ideal ambition. Dazzled by his new vision as well as by the sudden turn of external events, Rómulo, although apprehensive over the safety and welfare of his mistress, becomes expansive, contrary to his usual conduct as a mere gardener. Enjoying new freedom and his role as secret protector of Her Grace, he frequently visits her with one pretext or another. A creature of grace, unnatural yet somehow real, she by her enigmatic behavior, often childlike or irrational, dismays and torments her passionate protector. She insists, for example, despite the obvious dangers to her safety, on having clandestine visitors in her tower hideaway almost nightly: first the Duke until he is captured by Rómulo and executed shortly thereafter when turned over to the militiamen, and later Esteban, a dissolute marquis who is fighting for the Rebels and who is a faithful personification of cynicism and evil. The Duchess laugh-

ingly refers to Esteban as the *diablo,* and writes in her diary
that he is the very antithesis of Rómulo. "'Esteban jeers at everything . . . and Rómulo admires and reveres everything'" (126).
Obviously Rómulo and Esteban represent antithetical moral
positions in life.

As the bloody siege of Madrid continues, circumstances (shell
fire and bombardments which damage the top floors, the approach of winter) obligate Her Grace to descend the tower floor
by floor. On the sociopsychological level her descent is symbolic of her progress in human understanding—from aristo-
cratic aloofness and superficiality to the common level of universal humanity, as Robert Heilman was the first to observe.[5]

One night Esteban, while visiting the Duchess, momentarily
turns on powerful lights from the tower which illuminate the
palace grounds. The lights serve to guide Nationalist planes and
are followed immediately by a bombardment of the palace which
results in the death of forty-eight militiamen and Balbina,
Rómulo's conventional and ignorant wife. Although dismayed
over the passive complicity of his Lady in the bombardment,
her frivolity, indifference, and duplicity, Rómulo still worries
about her safety. Yet, since she persists in endangering her neck,
he feels that there is little that he can do and so he leaves for
the battle front, immediately distinguishing himself in combat
in which he destroys several enemy tanks. After a few days,
having been wounded in the leg, he returns to the palace
where he is acclaimed a hero. Except for this brief moment
of combat, the story ends with neither Rómulo nor the Duchess
ever having stirred from the palace—an outward immobility that
heightens the interior, subjective nature of the drama.

Upon his return the gardener resumes his clandestine visits
with the Duchess. Soon, however, he is mysteriously tricked
into believing that she has escaped to Valencia and safety.
Despondent, he stops going to the tower. Weeks later, however,
on a winter day, the palace now in almost total shambles—an
outward destruction which contrasts with a certain inner construction of the new Rómulo—he wanders into the second floor
of the tower to find Her Grace dying of a fever. Expiring in
Rómulo's arms, she summons her final strength to tell him:
"'You're the first man I've ever known in all my life'" (228).

Noblewoman and plebeian at last meet on the level of their common humanity. Overlaying this sociopsychological theme is the deeper one of man's need for an absolute ideal. The Duchess is Rómulo's illusion—his Queen. The ideal (one's dream of himself) must be pursued, but full possession of it must always be denied. An aphorism in the old ducal library, "For to attain ambition is to slay the same, and to realize therein the ambition of self-ideal is beyond the power of man, save by passing through death and misfortune" (183), explains the death of the Duchess, just when full realization of his ideal seems to be within Rómulo's grasp. The union or marriage of the concrete (Rómulo) and the abstract (the Duchess) can never be absolutely complete. Thus ends the story.

I *Rómulo's Quest*

Now let us look more closely at Rómulo's private quest. Since the pool scene Rómulo begins to feel like somebody else "and the need of understanding 'that other somebody'—which meant a brutal surprise—prevented him from knowing what he saw" (9). Clearly "that other somebody" is his ideal self, his dream of himself. "In his imagination, the Rómulo he had glimpsed at the swimming pool and still did not understand was being born, ripening, trying to grow and spread. It was not a completely new vision. He had known that Rómulo when he was about nineteen or twenty" (13). In his preoccupation with the "practical" affairs of life the middle-aged gardener had forgotten to gaze at the stars, had lost his youthful idealism.

In Senderian terminology, the ideal reality glimpsed in the pool scene by Rómulo can be identified in the terminology of *The Sphere*, as we saw in the last chapter, with "ganglionic reality," the abyss from which the Jebusite received his revelation, and the abode of *hombría* or the "man," as opposed to the "person." The terms "ganglia" and "person," however, are specifically not employed in *The King*: here the deeper reality becomes the source of "rebirth" and of recovery of one's early self-ideal. Rómulo's quest of his ideal self (the absolute ideal) began with his admission into a secret "reality" (the nudity of the Duchess).

In the larger social scene represented by the war, Rómulo imagines that the soldiers, too, are fighting " 'to get back their past, their lost lives, and in such a great getting back there's bound to be blood' " (166). Obviously, by their "past, their lost lives" Rómulo (Sender) means the deformation of their true humanity by an unjust and twisted social organization as well as by their own ignoble choice to serve the interests of the temporal "person" at the expense of the human species and of their own dimension toward the eternal, their "essential selves," *hombría*. Indirectly then—through an implied parallel between Rómulo and the Spanish masses—the novel is a commentary on the Civil War.

Though troubled by the Duchess's complicity with the Rebels, Rómulo remains loyal to her; the ideal must be placed above all partisan interests. " 'Nothing in the world matters so much as My Lady's safety' " (155). After the bombardment of the palace grounds, which easily could have resulted in death not only to the Republican militiamen but also to the Duchess as well, Rómulo is more worried than ever. " 'If suspicions gather round what the sentry said about "a stream of light," Her Grace is lost. They'll [the Republicans] kill her. And, if they kill her, the whole world—do you hear, My Lady?—the whole world'll be lost, too' " (153–54). He recognizes that the Loyalists might sacrifice the Ideal—and if they do, "the whole world'll be lost." Civilization is absolutely dependent on idealism.

But if Rómulo needs the Duchess, it is also true that she needs Rómulo. She confides to him, as outer circumstances darken: " 'Rómulo, you see what's happening. Violence and crime are already closing in on us forever, and I need you quiet, serene, capable of saving yourself and saving me' " (159). She asks him to " 'be stronger than all the madness around us' " (158). Without idealists there would be no idealism. Her Grace is only a dream—only a subjective creation in Rómulo's imagination, having no objective existence, an illusion. Essentially, then, the Duchess is an objectivization of Rómulo's subjective reality (and looked at this way, the technique here employed by Sender is expressionistic) just as the Jebusite in *The Sphere* is an objectivization of irrational, subliminal forces breaking out upon the surface of life.

Fantasizing that people may live on other "stars" and that from those "worlds" they look at the planet Earth and dream that everything here is perfect, Rómulo concludes: " 'Those people who dream about us are right. The things that are happening here, the things that are being accomplished now because we've got them in our blood, the things we're getting back—those are the very things they're dreaming about. Everything round us is just as beautiful as they believe it is' " (124–25). Beauty is merely in "the eyes of the beholder." " 'Everything round us is just as beautiful as they believe it is.' " Things are being accomplished because somehow we have them in our *blood*. A bleak, strange and mysterious fatalism or impersonal, mechanistic interpretation of total reality is suggested here. And yet Rómulo clings desperately to some kind of irrational faith in the Duchess. In a violent scene he, in a fit of jealousy, rips her coat off. As she stands frightened and naked from the waist up, he addresses her: " 'Yes. That's better. I've seen your body before, and from it—from this flesh, and these eyes that are frightened now and were mocking a moment ago—comes the light that makes everything more beautiful here than in other worlds. In those worlds they dream of us. Of you and me. They dream of me, too. Of me, seeing you naked now' " (152). Rómulo did not *really* see the Duchess half-naked—he, we must suppose, merely imagined or dreamed that he saw her. In the pool scene he looked at her, but "unseeingly." The ideal ambition is always beyond one's grasp. Its inaccessibility is poetically illustrated throughout *The King* in passages such as the following:

Rómulo came nearer, and she [the Duchess] drew back.
"I'm not a woman, Rómulo." (151)
He was still advancing, and she was retreating. (152)
She . . . said to herself: ". . . He seems to have chased me out of those rooms up there, and now I've come down to these other ones, running away and waiting. Running away from him. And waiting for him." (100)

When finally Rómulo holds the dead Duchess, now his "Queen," in his arms, he cries out in anguish: " 'Why now? . . . Why only now? . . . Does it have to be that way? Am I only to have you that way? When you no longer have yourself? Why?

Is it the law? The ancient law?' . . . Nobody answered him" (229).

Yet, despite the desolate ending, all is not lost. As the chaos and misery of the war increase, so does Rómulo's comprehension of the "reality" of the Duchess. Though he finds that his hopes in her are without logical foundation, and that she almost nightly entertains a criminal, the "devil" Esteban, in her apartment, he prefers to cling to his illusion: " 'If the duchess were really as she thinks she is, I wouldn't do what I'm doing for her' " (197). Strangely enough, in the midst of "blood, death, crime and war" (171) he observes that " 'the duchess seems stronger than ever' " (171). Outward catastrophe can lead individuals to discover within themselves "deeper" realities—"ganglionic" realities—in which they find new inspiration for living. Faith, "the assurance of things hoped for, the conviction of things not seen,"[6] often seems to be born and to thrive just when outer circumstances are least conducive to a natural optimism.

Rómulo's "spiritual" growth is manifested in his new attitudes. His former acute consciousness of everyday reality, for example, becomes dimmed. In the presence of His Lady he asks " 'War, fire, blood, what do they matter to us, to you and me?' " (122). It should be noticed that he says "to us, to you and me," not simply "to me." He needed the absolute ideal. His heroism at "Rómulo's Rock" sprang directly from his devotion to Her Grace; he tells her: " 'I'm willing to offer my head in place of Her Grace's, if it comes to losing it. But I won't offer it for anybody else's' " (160). His increasing indifference to the outer realities of existence (in favor of inner realities) does not imply a growing callousness. Though the condition of society was sad, "lamentable," he muses, an individual man must still make choices. " 'War, blood, what are they?' " " 'I don't mean it isn't sad, but over and above all this I've got my own way to make. A new way, My Lady' " (122).

The author states that Rómulo's "need of understanding 'that other somebody' " that he had glimpsed at the pool scene would mean for him "a brutal surprise" (9). Probably the heaviest import of that "brutal surprise" falls upon Rómulo as he finally realizes the impossibility of the consummation of his love affair, as he learns that "that other somebody" was ultimately only an illusion. Yet, he learns more; he discovers progressively, at the cost of great mental anguish, that in Her Grace's reality the terms "good" and "evil," "moral" and "immoral," have no meaning. He finds out that the Duchess—a symbol not only of ideal ambition, but also of absolute reality itself—is utterly indifferent to human joy or sorrow.

As seen in our discussion of *The Sphere*, on the level of the Duchess, morality, as ordinarily understood, is without validity. There are many passages I might cite from *The King* in support of this assertion, but let the following meditation by Her Grace suffice: " 'He's [Rómulo] a criminal, but there's a sort of innocence in him. I'm as guilty of the duke's death as he is. And yet at the same time I'm innocent, too. But if we're all innocent, where does the crime come from? Who hatches it, and where, and what for?' " (123). Even crime is part and parcel of Absolute Reality, and since the Absolute by definition must be perfect, then crime itself becomes "innocence." Such "poetic" reasoning is typical of Sender's work, a confusion of levels done more for poetic rather than for philosophical-logical reasons. To accept such statements as strictly philosophical rather than poetic-philosophical would be like trying to describe a beefsteak in terms of electrons, neutrons, and protons. A beefsteak may be one thing at one level and another at another, but not both on the same level—as a naively literal interpretation of the above and similar passages might imply; one cannot be both guilty and innocent, for example, on the same level (though he may be morally innocent and yet legally guilty). To those who believe there is no guilt there, of course, can be no innocence; all is amoral.

If we are to take the novel seriously on its deepest level, we must ask the question: If the absolute ideal, i.e., the Ideal, is finally only an illusion, what is to save man from cosmic despair? There are always two opposite positions in Sender's works: " 'Everything in life is nothing,' " meditates Rómulo, and Sender the author adds: "But life was a jumble of vice-versas, and the contrary could also be said. Anything, the most insignificant thing, is everything in life" (135). The fact that Rómulo undergoes a remarkable personal transformation for the better—becomes an authentic man and a "king," not a mere servitor—in his pursuit of the Ideal is an exaltation of the value of idealism

in and of itself, a glorification of climbing the mountain for the
sake of the climb itself, not for reaching the top of the mountain. Yet if the Duchess—the Ideal (and yet only an illusion)—
is lost, "the whole world'll be lost." For all his pains Rómulo,
like Don Quixote, is never allowed full possession of the object
of his devotion, and the haunting question still remains: By
such assertions as "the ideal is only an illusion," does Sender
really mean to make a final or dogmatic philosophical statement
about reality? Hardly, for he has always spurned dogmatism
except for what amounts to dogma with him: that in final matters
nothing for certain can ever be known, or verified.

If idealism is ultimately based upon a lie, i.e., if it finally has
no independent, objective, and transcendent reality as opposed
to subjective reality, man would not have a rational basis for
an optimistic interpretation of Life (Ultimate Reality). Sender,
however, going beyond the limitations of the strictly logical,
both in his writing and in his personal life, continues to express
both despair *and* hope. He leaves it to the reader to arrive at
his own synthesis, or to take an affirmative or negative position.
In the same world exist both the devilish marquis, Esteban, and
the idealistic peasant, Rómulo. The Duchess is beyond both
of them, encompassing both the world of the marquis and of
the gardener, and in this way symbolizing the final "what" of
things; she is on a level on which morality, as commonly understood, is, in Sender's view, without validity. Yet on her realistic
or human plane she expresses ideas that are antithetical to those
of the gardener. For example, when Rómulo, in the midst of
destruction, affirms that he is " 'beginning to realize there's
always something fond and loving behind even the most horrible things, something stronger, and higher that saves us . . .
that evil would never have the last word,' " the Duchess continues to smile: " 'No. There's always a greater evil. And after
the most horrible evil we can imagine, there's no loving reason
at all, only a huge roar of laughter' " (148). Obviously the
author does not side definitively with either of these opposing
positions; his real attitude is skeptical of both—a "synthesis" of
two logically opposite views. Expressive of the ambivalent manner and message of *The King* is its conclusion. Just as the
Duchess has expired in Rómulo's arms, Queen Hypotenuse the

puppet seems to sing out: " 'And from the shadows to the great light' " (230). But Rómulo (modern man) "did not know whether he had heard 'the great light,' or 'the great night,' or the blight or the plight or the fight or perhaps the kite or the bite. . ." (231).

Thus, the reader is left free to believe that the universe is utterly absurd or that there is ultimate meaning and sense in life, to choose between despair or hope, pessimism or optimism. But on what basis may he hope? On some mystical intuitive "knowledge" granted to him alone? Or shall he make some kind of Kierkegaardian leap of faith, or arbitrarily affirm "faith in faith" as did Unamuno? Can an intelligent man be satisfied merely with subjective or intuitive evidence—as opposed to objective, verifiable evidence—that Final Reality sustains him or does not sustain him in his noblest notions of what life *ought* to be? Sender, as does the prevailing intellectualism of this century, rejects out of hand all absolutes in favor of relativism. Without some presuppositions about the nature of Ultimate Reality man cannot, of course, even speculate about final questions. Beginning with only *rationalistic* presuppositions (by which I mean that system of thought which begins with man alone and limits all efforts to find final meaning to life to that which does not go beyond man—what is sometimes known as philosophical humanism) all theories about final matters must of necessity be regarded as relative and subjective, not objective. Twentieth-century man is caught in this closed circle. Answers to the final questions which save life from absurdity lie outside the rationalistic circle; they are declared "off-limits" to the objective mind. Yet modern man rebels against the impossible restrictions of this closed system; among writers the rebellion can be seen in an emphasis upon the unconscious, including an interest in mysticism and the occult. In Western society growing numbers of people seek escape from a universe without transcendental meaning by "dropping out" of the mainstream of society and experimentation with drugs and irrational mysticism.

Yet despite the relativism that dominates the thinking of this century, it is *not unreasonable* to believe in absolutes, though such a belief is not *rationalistic* (as I defined rationalistic above). A *reasonable* or *rational* presupposition about the final nature of reality, for example, is that God, or an Unmoved Mover, if you like, created all that is. Finding this presupposition reasonable, we may then find it entirely reasonable to suppose that such a Being could be "personal" in nature (as well as impersonal), and that being personal He might wish to communicate with personal man, etc. On such rational (not rationalistic) premises one may build a world view which allows belief in absolute values, thus providing a unified view of truth, a view which has no radical discontinuity between the rational and the transcendental or religious, or between reason and faith (though faith is not an exercise of reason, it may be firmly based upon what is reasonable). Such a unified view of truth or of life seems to be the desired goal of Sender's metaphysical speculations, yet such nonrationalistic (but *reasonable*) premises, as stated above, are especially suspect to the author because of their failure to make man the "measure of all things," and perhaps because of their propagation by the Roman Catholic Church and Christian sectarians. Don Ramón, of course, is not alone; the rejection of belief in absolutes by the leading intelligentsia and literati of this century has been almost total. The majority of Existentialists, especially Jean-Paul Sartre and Albert Camus, who have exerted the strongest influence upon European intellectuals in the mid-twentieth century, have, for example, spurned all Judeo-Christian presuppositions about Reality, assuming that life is irrational, absurd, chaotic, and finally meaningless. Sender, by comparison with Sartre, appears almost to be an optimist or an orthodox believer in God; he keeps speaking of "faith," of the unity of all mankind, of the "ideal," etc. Yet it is hard to see why his "God" (actually not "God" but a "God-word"), a Blind Universal Impersonal Force, can, despite all literary posing, be the ground for greater hope than Sartre's nothingness.

If we apply classic logic, the first formula of which is "If you have A it is not non-A," Sender's theological-philosophical positions lead to despair. If, for example, A, "God exists," is true, then its opposite, B, "God does not exist," is *not true*. Classic logic, however, is rejected by Sender in favor of the Hegelian dialectic; thus, Sender's position is neither A nor B, but C: "God *may* exist." Indeed, acceptance of only the tentative

synthesis is an important key to understanding Sender's thought
and art. The dramatic tension and dynamic quality of *The King*,
as indeed of Sender's entire literary work, are largely achieved
by a vacillation in viewpoint, sometimes moving toward the
thesis and sometimes toward the antithesis, toward the positive,
then the negative side of the central synthesis: "The absolute
ideal *may* exist" (in *The King*). At the end of *The King* we
are left with grey doubt, not with a black or white "answer."
Sender never abandons himself to despair; he clings, as it were,
to Tennyson's "sunnier side of doubt." In the human situation
he finds, as did Rómulo, much that would lead him to despair,
but much as did Baroja, at the bottom of it all he is always
able to find something that would lead him to affirm hope or
faith—albeit arbitrarily. And one may find cause for hope, de-
pending, of course, on his own presuppositions regarding life,
in the primary thesis of the novel, expressed in the following
"poetic idea" discovered by the Duchess in the book from the
ducal library, *Examples of Monarchies*: " 'The universe is an
immense monarchy. We, as dwellers in the universe, must fatally
submit to it, and in our turn, are kings of that reality which
makes up our existence. Everything which man has dreamed,
dared, created, has been done because of this monarchy of
man—king—and his illusion—queen. Man—the king—and his
ideal ambition—the queen' " (182–83). We recognize in *The
King* the old story of Don Quixote. Comments Donald Barr:
"[*The King and the Queen*] ends tragically, private tragedy in
the midst of public tragedy, as is appropriate to the tragic sense
of life so firmly rooted in the center of the Spanish vision. But
it ends exultantly, for it exhibits the large firm space that dreams
can clear for themselves in the universal chaos of reality."[7]

II *The Duchess's Quest*

Not only Rómulo but the Duchess also was seeking self-
realization. Living a vain and shallow life with the Duke whom
she did not love, she no doubt subconsciously felt the need for
a man who would awaken her to the passionate potentialities
within her own personality. The Duke, "a man incapable of
passions" (8), and dominated by the Duchess is, in Sender's

terms, more "person" than "man." The Duchess instinctively, but unconsciously, recognizes her gardener as more "man" than "person" and therefore capable of fulfilling her as a woman. Robert Heilman affirms:

It is possible to state the duchess's problem in this way: the search for self-realization is intertwined with the effort to recognize and encompass manliness—. . . . Her exposure of her body to Rómulo, at the beginning of the story, is on one level of course what she takes it to be—a gesture of contempt toward one who is "not a man"; yet it is also an expression of an unformed desire to be seen and known in some more essential way than she has hitherto experienced ("Things happen to the duchess like in dreams," a servant says; this dreamlike act is a declaration of a need not admitted in full consciousness). Her act is a challenge—a challenge which evokes a sexual response; the latter is identified with the resurgence of "blood" and "youth" in Rómulo . . . the story moves from psychological exploration into metaphysical speculation.[8]

Her Grace progressively descends from the surface or "person" level of life to a deeper level represented by the "blood" and "youth" of Rómulo. It is this deeper level of life—the subconscious or "ganglionic"—which in the ultimate analysis determines her enigmatic behavior throughout the novel, in the end leading her to recognize true "manhood" in Rómulo—a long journey from her derisive and supercilious "Rómula a man?" (9). Essentially, then, Rómulo becomes recognized as her ideal just as she is his.

III Summation

The King is essentially the story of Rómulo's intimate quest for the Absolute Ideal, effectively damatized against the background of the Spanish Civil War. The story is told from the point of view of the omniscient author. The author's own comments often subtly merge with those of Rómulo, who obviously represents Sender himself. Sender, now as Sender-Rómulo, now as Sender-author, keeps firm control from beginning to end. Straightforward narrative prevailing over a minimum of description gives the work a generally dynamic character. Though the speech and conduct of the Duchess are realistic, the author has avoided direct physical description of her; any such description would have detracted from Sender's central purpose—to portray her as a lovely creature of the imagination, and thus symbolic of the Absolute Ideal.

The poetic dimension is sought through Rómulo's poetic-philosophical musings; the juxtaposition of the monstrous and the beautiful (Esteban and the Duchess), the grotesque and the ideal (Midge, the deformed dwarf who fights off giant rats in the basement of the tower inhabited by the Duchess); the puppets which seem to come alive and comment on the central story of Rómulo and the Duchess; the symbolism itself of the narrative; the delicate shading of fantasy and reality which produces a dreamlike atmosphere; the element of mystery and surprise; the use of metaphor and of motif (e.g., renaissance, the nakedness of the Duchess, etc.). In truth, *The King* is another Senderian novel written *sub species poetica*. Together Rómulo and the Duchess represent a microcosm of all humanity: "'Together the two of them form the monarchy that rules over the universe'" (164).

More successfully than in any other Senderian novel, with the possible exception of *A Man's Place* and *Requiem for a Spanish Peasant*, the sociopolitical and the personal are woven together here to create an artistic unity; indeed, the collective and the individual seem to be different angles of the same reality. Likewise one could say that the three distinct levels of the narrative —the realistic-melodramatic, the sociopsychological, and the lyrical-metaphysical—seem to reinforce rather than conflict with one another. Allegorical meaning and realistic story detract only minimally, if at all, from each other. There is unity of theme and story, continuity of mood and time. The strange combination of Rómulo's subjective reality with the outer, objective circumstances and events coalesce to form in the reader a special perspective in which the lyrical dimension finds ready welcome. Sender again shows himself here to be a master of natural dialogue. Above all, however, he knows human psychology and flawlessly creates for us Rómulo's peculiar psychological world, the world from which the reader gradually comes to view the larger world of the novel and which impregnates all with its own flavor or tone. The lyrical-metaphysical dimension does not become obscured but remains in the central position, thus contributing rather than detracting from the overall unity and intelligibility of the work. Symbolism harmonizes, rather than clashes, with the basic intentions of the novel. As mentioned earlier, opposing philosophical positions are maintained in dynamic equilibrium according to the Hegelian dialectic of thesis-antithesis; the reader is left to resolve the contradictions in his own tentative synthesis, or to reject the relativistic approach in favor of a belief in absolutes and the use of classical logic: "If you have A it is not non-A."

CHAPTER 7

Other Novels, 1939-1971

M Y purpose in this chapter is to review very briefly the many Senderian novels which have appeared during the author's exile and which I have not discussed in some detail in the preceding three chapters. Except for the historical novels which I group at the end of this chapter, I examine the works here in the order of their publication dates.

Sender's first postwar novel, *Proverbio de la muerte* (*Proverb of Death*), 1939, was later modified, extensively augmented, and given a new title, *La esfera* (*The Sphere*), 1947, by the author. Chapter 5 has been devoted to an analysis of this important work.

I *Nonhistorical Novels*

A. Epitalamio del prieto Trinidad (Dark Wedding)

Epitalamio del prieto Trinidad (*Black Trinidad's Nuptial Song*, given the title *Dark Wedding* for its English translation), 1942, is one of Sender's best novels. Its plot is simple. Black Trinidad, the sinister but somehow likeable boss or warden of Faro Island, a penal colony in the Caribbean, travels to the capital on the mainland where he marries a young and innocent girl less than half his age, Niña Lucha. Immediately after the wedding reception Trinidad, uneasy in the city, insists on flying at once with his bride—still in her wedding dress—to the Island. In the riotous welcome given the newly-married couple upon their arrival, Trinidad, angered by the noisy and vulgar demonstrations, impulsively shoots and kills two convicts. That night, as he prepares to enter the nuptial chamber, he is murdered by an unknown assailant. The novel having thus far maintained a sober and realistic style—in fact, realism at Sender's very best—now gradually moves into a dreamlike world of semi-

123

reality and semifantasy, and its symbolic nature becomes visible. Trinidad's death sets off a confused struggle among the depraved and crazed convicts for control of the island and possession of the "little widow," who now symbolizes the absolute ideal: "All this—truth, beauty, the ineffable harmony—was nothing but the girl [Niña]."[1] While the two factions vying for power roam the island clashing and killing, Niña is hidden in a cave by Darío, a young idealistic schoolteacher and the only decent man on the island.

In the end, the inmates of the prison colony, in an implicit recognition of the sacrificial heroism exhibited by Darío who risked his life by running through a wall of fire to rescue the virgin-widow, agree to allow the schoolteacher to take her to the mainland. But as the launch carrying them leaves Faro Island Darío looks back and says:

> "Perhaps we should go back and do something for those people."
> The girl agreed, perhaps to obey Darío, or perhaps because of the idea itself.
> "Yes," Darío said. "Let's go back. If somebody doesn't help them they're lost."[2]

Darío orders the motorman to return them to the island. In refusing to leave the island, obviously they—the idealist and the ideal—are refusing to turn their backs on the plight of mankind.

Mark Schorer complains: "The manipulation of events at the end seems arbitrary—an assertion of the author's good will rather than the final assertion of the novel itself."[3] It should be kept in mind that Sender's "good will" does not spring from a facile optimism, but from an intuitive faith in the essential goodness of reality despite appearances, and even the hopelessness which seems inherent in his philosophical position (discussed especially in Chapters 5 and 6 of this study). Yet unless one accepts the philosophical view of life made visible throughout *Dark Wedding*, principally through the thoughts and internal monologues of Darío, the author's alter ego, as an essential part of "the final assertion of the novel itself," Schorer's criticism is justified for the "good" represented by Darío and Niña seems more often to be crucified in real life than to emerge victorious. But in Sender's view, even if the "good" is crucified it is somehow "victorious." An important principle expressed by Darío is that "life is an ideal in process."[4] All of humanity is part and parcel of this "ideal in process"—Life. The idealistic urge is inherent in life. Darío's ontward success at the end of the novel is merely symbolic of his inner satisfaction or success. He realizes that he can never fully possess the ideal absolute—the virgin —but he finds fulfillment as a man in pursuing the ideal, the unreachable star. The girl, Niña, asserts her faith that " 'everything that lives is beautiful, if we know how to look at it. Beauty is not in things but in our hearts.' "[5]

Several critics have noticed a certain Valleinclanesque flavor and atmosphere in *Dark Wedding*; indeed, there is similarity in atmosphere with Valle-Inclán's novel of an American dictator, *Tirano Banderas* (*The Tyrant Banderas*). In some of the scenes there is also an esperpentic and nightmarish quality which recalls *Divinas palabras* (*Divine Words*) as well as the Galician writer's *esperpentos*. The following description of a weird *post mortem* wedding feast for Trinidad (the name, "Trinity," is obviously symbolic of power—the Godhead and the church, state, and army of Spain) the night after his having been murdered is somewhat reminiscent of Valle-Inclán as well as illustrative of the poetic vein of the book:

Rosin torches fastened to the trees threw out a leaping light. Baskets of tortillas, skins full of pulque, and flour and corn-meal tidbits were brought in. The hubbub increased as new groups arrived. Around that circle the night breathed harsh and black. There was hardly room for people to move. From far off came the sound of the sea. The lanterns gave a blue light and the torches red, the lanterns casting on the face the spell of a water-front brothel. In one corner Spitball was making his public debut with the polka, *Shoot Pepe,* on the accordion.[6]

Poetic or subjective elements in the above passage include the following: "leaping light," "night breathed harsh and black," the feeling of being pressed together in the crowd, the distant "sound of the sea," the blue light of the lanterns, the red light of the torches, "the spell of a water-front brothel," and the eccentric character, Spitball, playing the accordion.

Characterization in the novel is weak, a weakness inherent in the author's purpose and method. The characters, even Darío and Niña, are more symbols of abstractions than they are real persons. The physical appearance of Niña, for example, is never described in any concrete or realistic manner, yet she becomes a lovely creature of the imagination. Her sexual power is only implied. Narrative interest, aided by intense melodrama (an aesthetic weakness), is sustained throughout the book. *Dark Wedding* has also appeared in translation in German, Swedish, Danish, Portuguese, and Czech. It was reprinted in Spanish in 1966, in Spain, thus becoming available to the readers of Spain for the first time, twenty-four years after its original appearance in Mexico.

B. El verdugo afable (The Affable Hangman)

Sender's next novel not discussed in preceding chapters was *El verdugo afable* (*The Affable Hangman*), 1952, an ambitious work in which the author includes material from his prewar trilogy: *Public Order, Trip to the Village of Crime,* and *The Night of One Hundred Heads,* discussed in Chapter 3, along with much new material. It is a kind of "summing up" or recapitulation of Sender's art and thought; it is both simple and complex, realistic and laden with *conceptista* allegory; its flatly reportorial tone oscillates with the fantastic, the hallucinatory, the imaginative, imbuing the whole with a dreamlike atmosphere and symbolic meaning. It should be noted that the English translation of *The Affable Hangman* which appeared in 1963 is not just a translation but a substantial revision of the original Spanish edition, with many omissions, some additions, and other changes. An important change is in the time of the action: during the twenties in the original Spanish version, and from that time on into the Civil War and beyond in the English. *The Affable Hangman* is about a quarter less extensive than the Spanish text and is aesthetically—despite a poor translation—an improvement.

The Affable Hangman is the biography of one Ramiro Vallemediano, a Spanish garroter, as told to the journalist, Juan Echenique (who in the Spanish appears as Ramón Sender himself). In effect, the novel becomes an analysis of the executioner's soul and way of viewing life, of how he came to assume willingly the position of public executioner, and all this against the vivid backdrop of a decadent Spanish society. Ramiro began his life as a bastard; he drifted from one thing to another, remaining always on the "margin" of life, unwilling to integrate himself into the social system, which he saw as false and degrading. He came to embrace the ideals of Miguel Molinos, the quietest who preached a nonengagement with The World. "If there is some purity in me," he writes, "it is only that of the man on the margin."[7] Eventually Ramiro, a victim and reject of society, comes to offer himself as a martyr to preserve that society. In a letter he writes: "I sometimes think that there is only one man who lives the truth and who, furthermore, deserves the gratitude of all the rest and does not ask for it: the hangman. Upon his head rests all the social order known until today, and still the hangman, aware of it, offers himself as a propitious object for the scorn, fear, and moral repugnance of all. Here is the martyr and hero, and the man who can be a smiling hero and martyr, because he has found the truth."[8] The ultimate irony is that Ramiro, the "marginal" man or escapist, should take upon himself responsibility for a vile and false society, to stand at what he regarded as the apex of the pyramid of law and order.

Comments Hilary Corke: *"The Affable Hangman* is not a shocker or *roman noir,* but a serious philosophical essay upon responsibility, upon refusal, upon the question as to whether, laboring under the certainty of mortality, it is desirable or not to enter upon the busy life of the world. It is, as I have said, a peculiarly Spanish essay."[9] James Gray writes: "This deeply disturbing book is desperately in earnest about the challenges it puts before present-day society. It is always thoughtful, often brilliant. One feels oneself to be, throughout the reading, in the presence of a major intelligence and a valiant spirit."[10] For lack of space it is impossible here even to begin to consider properly the many fascinating concepts in this densely written novel nor to assess its fine poetic realism, unified structure, and

other literary qualities. A masterful analysis of its themes and
techniques can be read in Spanish in Marcelino C. Peñuelas's
book, *La obra narrativa de Ramón J. Sender.*

C. Los cinco libros de Ariadna (The Five Books of Ariadne)

The Five Books of Ariadne appeared in 1957, two years after
the first of its five "books" had been published as a separate
novel with the title *Ariadna.* The substance of this long novel
of 584 pages centers around the treacherous dealings of the
Soviets on the Republican front during the Spanish Civil War,
although an effort to recreate the moral climate of not only the
war but of the period immediately prior to 1936 is made. The
novel begins without warning on a surrealistic plane: the con-
vening of the Twenty-Seventh Assembly of the OMECC, a world
organization reminiscent of the United Nations, to examine
the causes and conduct of the Spanish Civil War. The Assembly
becomes an allegory itself. The two principal personages are
Javier, who is obviously Sender, and Ariadne, his lover. Both
give their testimonies, which occupy a substantial part of the
novel, before the Assembly presided over by a mysterious personage who either never arrives or who is invisible.

Sender has said that almost everything in *The Five Books
of Ariadne* "is autobiographical." "Of course," he continued,
"one has to add fantasy and imagination to make it more effective, but it is autobiographical, especially on the moral
plane."[11] Josefa Rivas writes that the work "tries to capture the
fundamental aspects and the deepest reasons of the Spanish
drama and, through the incongruences narrated, it succeeds
in conveying an idea of the situation of Spain at that historical
moment."[12] The book does indeed recreate the moral climate
or *ambiente* of the Spanish conflict, aggravated by the Soviet
and Fascist interventions. Sender has called it "a bloody satire
against the Stalinists and against the Fascists."[13] It is that, of
course, but it attempts to be more; it is a very complex novel
that moves on different levels, frequently abruptly changing
the time, place, and narrative point of view with what appear
at times to the befuddled reader to be capricious and annoying
digressions; indeed, the very chaos of the situation narrated

seems to be simulated. The work suffers from a profusion of material which has only an obscure relation, if any, to its main narrative substance.

There are some passages which recall *Contraataque* (translated as *Counter-Attack in Spain*), Sender's book of personal narrative of the war written in the midst of hostilities, yet *The Five Books of Ariadne* is an entirely new book: the conflict examined in retrospect by Sender nineteen years later. As such it is valuable as testimonial literature and as a study of the Spanish mind; except for this value, however, it adds little, if anything, to Sender's stature as a writer.

D.   Emen hetan (Here We Are)

In *Emen hetan* (*Here We Are*), 1958, a witches' sabbath on the eve of St. John's Day in the Basque area of Spain during the eighteenth century serves Sender as a pretext for expatiating on a disconcerting theme: Spain is the land of Satan. Both the thesis and the tone in which it is developed seem to deny Don Ramón's lifelong love for his native country, so evident in the bulk of his literary work; perhaps *Here We Are* was composed during a period of depression and possible bitterness or despair at the trend of events in Spain almost two decades after the Civil War. Josefa Rivas observed that the novel "is imbued with bad faith of the same kind that impregnates the film, *Viridiana,* conceived and directed by Luis Buñuel."[14] It is especially vicious in its attack upon the Catholic Church; altogether—with its scabrous humor, sophistry, tiresome repetition, and lack of narrative thrust—the work must be judged a failure. Nevertheless, with only minor adaptations, it was later incorporated into one of Sender's best historical novels, *Las criaturas saturnianas* (*The Saturnine Creatures*), 1968.

E.   Los laureles de Anselmo (The Laurels of Anselm)

In reality more drama than novel is Sender's *Los laureles de Anselmo* (*The Laurels of Anselm*), 1958. Except for a long passage concluding Chapter 10 and a short narrative-explanatory passage beginning each of its twelve chapters, the book consists of dialogue. Revealing Sender's continued interest in the nature of reality, *The Laurels of Anselm* is an imaginative re-creation of Calderón's seventeenth-century masterpiece, *Life is a Dream*, set in a large industrial North American city in the present century.

Having been drugged, Anselm, an impecunious sewer worker, is carried off while in a deep sleep and left in the elegant home of the financial tycoon who had illegitimately begotten him some thirty years before and who now wishes to make amends by legally recognizing Anselm and making him heir to his fortune. On awakening from his drug-induced sleep and find-ing himself, as it were, in a "new world" and with a changed station in life, Anselm questions the reality of what is happen-ing to him; he begins to act as if he were dreaming, accom-plishing with ease that which formerly had been impossible or exceedingly difficult.

Despite its poetic-philosophical musings which make inter-esting reading, a certain dramatic quality in the situation, and sprightly dialogue the work does not create an aesthetic unity. As Marra-López writes, it is a strange mixture—not fusion, but mixture—of reality and fantasy. Marra-López sees in it an unsatisfactory product of the author's constant searching for new narrative forms.[15]

F. La luna de los perros (The Moon of the Dogs)

A much better novel than *The Laurels of Anselm* is *La luna de los perros* (*The Moon of the Dogs*), 1962, in which Rafael Parga, a Spanish exile, recalls his somber experiences in Paris during the murky days of the German occupation in 1941. The bleak moral climate of Paris at that time, as well as the despera-tion of the protagonist (who resembles Saila in *The Sphere*), prevails throughout the book, which opens with the following: "I am alone. In December the sun sets at four in the afternoon. The night is long and the wind moans in the chimney like an ox."[16]

Beginning in the present, Rafael soon jumps back in memory to his experiences of a few months previously, centering for the most part around his strange and ambivalent feelings and relationships with his lover, the enigmatic Raquel, to whom he is drawn and repelled at the same time. In the end he kills her to rid himself of his obsession, and the novel ends with Rafael's enjoying the companionship of Raquel's soul in his dreams; he now desires to live, having liberated himself from his suicidal urge through murder. In its recreation of the nihilistic mood and criminal atmosphere of occupied Paris in 1941, *The Moon of the Dogs* comes very near to being an Existentialist work. "In the end," comments Charles Olstad, "Parga [Rafael] reveals neither motivation nor repentance. His crime is simply an arbitrary gesture, as has been his repeated decision against suicide. Representative of a world with no discernible meaning, in which all vestiges of traditional morality are deliberately trampled, Parga seems to stand as an 'exemplary' hero in the ironic sense typified by Pascual Duarte (or by Sender's own *El verdugo afable*)."[17] "We are," writes Rafael Bosch, "like dogs barking at the moon (hence the title) and biting each other for no reason at all, but (different from existentialism) we are not responsible for it. The only fault lies with the chaotic world in which we live—a world which cheats and beats us and deprives our lives of sense and hope."[18] Though not autobiographical, *The Moon,* through its protagonist, Rafael Parga, reflects the author's own desperate search for meaning in love, in life, and in death. Rafael's memories are told in a dense, direct, terse, verbal style, and in the first person; as in most of Sender's novels there are obscure passages and references which lend an air of poetic mystery to the whole at times but which may also only disconcert or befuddle the reader.

G. La tesis de Nancy (Nancy's Thesis)

Sender's next novel, *La tesis de Nancy* (*Nancy's Thesis*), 1962, presents a humorous picture of Spain as seen through the eyes of Nancy, an American university student from Pennsylvania, who has gone to Andalusia to write her doctoral thesis in Spanish. Except for a short "Prior Note" to the reader, the novel consists of ten chapters, each a letter from Nancy to her cousin, Betsy, in the United States in which she relates her impressions of Spain and her adventures, romantic and otherwise. The result is entertaining while revealing the formidable cultural differences

which make difficult the way of Americans who seek to penetrate
the enigma which is Spain. The chief virtue of the book, Sender's only epistolary novel, lies in its poetic humor, a humor
which is not bitter nor raucous, but understanding and tolerant.

H.   El bandido adolescente (The Adolescent Bandit)

Sender's first novel to be published in Spain since *Mr. Witt
Among the Rebels* in 1936 was *El bandido adolescente* (*The
Adolescent Bandit*), 1965, the story of Billy the Kid, the outlaw
who gained notoriety for his crimes in the New Mexico Territory in the 1870's. It is the author's first and only novel with
a setting in New Mexico, Don Ramón's home state for more
than sixteen years. Although Sender has followed closely the
incidents related in *The Authentic Life of Billy, the Kid*, first
published in 1882 by Pat Garrett, the sheriff who killed the
outlaw, he has stamped his adaptation of the legend with his
own inimitable style and private interpretation. Garrett's account, a mixture of fact and fiction, is the foundation book of
the extensive Billy-the-Kid bibliography.

The virtues of saints, poets, and heroes have always interested Sender. There were elements of greatness in Billy the
Kid which lifted him above the ordinary. In Senderian terms,
there was something of the hero, of the saint, and of the poet
in the Kid. There are other reasons for Sender's interest. The
Kid, although usually in the company of others, was subjectively
and essentially alone, the existentialist individual, without past
or future. Somehow or other his reckless indifference to life
and death suggested that he knew values superior to either,
which were the source of his valor. He was a primitive man,
and represented "natural law" at a time and place undergoing
the birth pangs of law and order. The outlaw was every inch
a man, *muy macho*, but not in an erotic sense. Rather he looked
upon women much as did the knights of old. Born of Irish-
Catholic parents in New York City, the Kid grew up in New
Mexico and learned to speak Spanish well. The *hispanos* who
admired his gallantry with women, his daring deeds, and regarded him generally as their defender against the encroaching
anglos (typified by ruthless cattle ranchers) came to look

upon him as one of their own. Youth, manhood, idealism (in his own peculiar way), heroism—all essential Senderian qualities —were possessed by the Kid.

The Adolescent Bandit may be the first novel to be written by a Spaniard on the life of the great outlaw of the Southwest. J. C. Dyke's *Billy the Kid: The Bibliography of a Legend* (Albuquerque: University of New Mexico Press, 1952), the most comprehensive bibliography on the legend published to date, does not list a single item in Spanish. It lists a French novel on the Kid which appeared in 1889. Though not one of Sender's best novels, *The Adolescent Bandit* is a first-rate story, worth reading.

I. Crónica del alba (Chronicle of Dawn), Volumes I–III

In 1966 the three-volume, nine-part or nine-novel series, *Crónica del alba* (*Chronicle of Dawn*), whose first part appeared as a separate novel in 1942, was finally completed and published in its definitive text. The first part, which bears the title of the longer work, has already been considered in Chapter 4. The remaining eight parts, which can be discussed here in only the most summary fashion because of space limitations, bear the following titles: Volume I, *Hipogrifo violento* (*Violent Hippogriff*), *La quinta Julieta* (*The Villa Julieta*); Volume II, *El mancebo y los héroes* (*The Youth and the Heroes*), *La onza de oro* (*The Ounce of Gold*), *Los niveles del existir* (*The Levels of Existing*); Volume III, *Los términos del presagio* (*The Terms of the Presage*), *La orilla donde los locos sonríen* (*The Shore Where Madmen Smile*), and *La vida comienza ahora.* (*Life Begins Now*).

Volume I, Part 2, *Violent Hippogriff*, first appeared as a separate novel in 1954. It begins precisely where the first part of the series left off—with eleven-year-old Pepe Garcés in a Catholic boarding school in Reus, Catalonia. During the academic year which the story covers, Pepe learns to adapt himself to the regimented life of the school, awakens to unsuspected depths in his own being, and discovers new dimensions in reality. Once again the enormously vital theme of Calderón's *Life is a Dream* finds expression; the title itself is borrowed from the first verse of the Spanish playwright's drama. In the preface to the separate novel, Sender wrote: "In these pages one sees the author trying in vain to unveil an absolute reality accessible only to religion or poetry."[19] The title itself (a hippogriff is a fabulous winged animal, half horse and half griffin—a griffin is a cross between a lion and an eagle) is expressive of the author's poetic intention. Among critics the consenus seems to be that *Violent Hippogriff* and the remaining seven parts of the long novel somehow fail to achieve the high artistic level of its first part. Though the series is indeed uneven in literary qualities, there are pages in its remaining "novels" or parts which are surely among the very best that Sender has written. The author values the long novel as his most ambitious work and as perhaps superior to *A Man's Place*, *Dark Wedding*, *The King and the Queen*, and *The Affable Hangman*.[20]

The third part of the first volume, *The Villa Julieta*, appeared first as a long story in the magazine *Panoramas* in Mexico during the summer of 1957; later that year it was published as a separate novel. It is the story of Pepe's adventures in the "Villa," a kind of recreational park in suburban Zaragoza, during the summer upon his return home from the school in Reus. Pepe's inflated ideas of himself seen in Part One suffer further diminution as he confronts some of the harsh realities of the Spanish social complex.

The next part, *The Youth and the Heroes,* finds Pepe enrolled in the Institute in Zaragoza. As he becomes more and more involved in the struggle for social justice, he finds himself further estranged from his bourgeois family. The violent death met by Checa, a teen-age revolutionary who is one of the book's "heroes," in an altercation with the police weighs heavily upon Pepe's consciousness. His love for Valentina persists. *The Youth and the Heroes* is the last part of the series to appear first as a separate novel, in 1960.

The second part of Volume II, *The Ounce of Gold*, provides an interlude in Pepe's agitated life: he lives for awhile with his peasant grandfather in a village. The old man, full of wisdom and anecdotes, a memorable character who incarnates the unchanging values of the Aragonese villagers, quietly instructs the lad, Pepe. In the next part, *The Levels of Existing,* the scene shifts to a Spanish town where Pepe has gone to work as a pharmacist's assistant. Though not named, the town is Alcañiz where Sender worked in a pharmacy for about a year while completing his high school work by taking courses accredited by the Institute of Teruel but administered by educators in Alcañiz. At this time Pepe experiences the pleasures of carnal love, and finds a conflict between voluptuosity and his more ideal or "spiritual" love for Valentina, a dualism that is common in much of Spanish literature and life. He continues his revolutionary activities, but becomes so demoralized that *The Levels of Existing* ends with his unsuccessful attempt to commit suicide.

In Volume III Pepe Garcés progresses from full manhood in *The Terms of the Presage* and *The Shore Where Madmen Smile* to pass rapidly well into the Spanish Civil War in the third part, *Life Begins Now.* There are passages of true lyrical force in this third volume; Valentina returns in Pepe's memory with the force of a pure ideal, no longer an entity of flesh and blood, but a mysterious suggestion, a dream, a secret nostalgia for some "Lost Paradise," a longing sharpened by the ugly realities of the prelude to civil war and civil war itself. The very chaos of the situation seems to be reflected in the complex structure of this last volume which moves on different levels and has many dimensions; the sociopolitical scene is portrayed while Sender poetically probes the nature of reality and of the human personality; action on one level frequently symbolizes reality on one or more other levels. Moments of surreality sometimes merge or fuse with the level of ordinary consciousness, and vice versa. And again the author demonstrates his great talent for satire, a social satire that serves the secondary purpose of providing humorous relief for the reader.

J. Nocturno de los 14 (Nocturne of the 14)

A dreamlike atmosphere and sequence prevail in *Nocturno de los 14* (*Nocturne of the 14*), 1969, in which the first-person narrator is visited one stormy night by fourteen suicide victims, all friends or acquaintances of the narrator. José Díaz, one-time secretary of the Spanish Communist party; Ernest Toller, Helen Wilkinson, and Ernest Hemingway are among the fourteen with whom the narrator (the author) converses while alone that night in the home of the strange widow, Mumú, whose husband, Charlie, committed suicide three yeares previously. Neither Mumú, who is away on vacation, nor her dead husband ever appears.

The arrival of each suicide victim becomes the occasion for fantastic dialogue, rambling anecdotes, and commentaries by the narrator; the episodic and fragmentary structure seems to be a mere pretext for the author's musings on themes of special interest to him, e.g., the difficulties of exile, motives for suicide, the mysteries of life and death, and possible explanations for Charlie's suicide.

K.   En la vida de Ignacio Morel (In the Life of Ignacio Morel)

The careful construction of *En la vida de Ignacio Morel* (*In the Life of Ignacio Morel*), 1969, its penetrating psychological realism, its lyrical dimension, humor, and narrative interest make it a delight to read; it is not surprising that it was awarded the Planeta Prize for 1969 and that fifty-five thousand copies were printed for its first edition.

Ignacio Morel is essentially Sender. The style is simple, clear, direct, verbal; the story, told in the third person, is coherent and unified. Chronological time is followed throughout the nine chapters of the novel, each of the first seven chapters covering one day in the life of Ignacio, a professor in a lycée in a Parisian suburb; the eighth and ninth chapters further develop the repercussions of the death of Madame Saint-Julien who had expired under most unusual circumstances: while making love to Ignacio in a downtown Paris hotel, probably from a heart attack. The juxtaposition of lust and death brings to mind the great Galician author, Valle-Inclán.

The usual Senderian motifs are present, adding depth and interest to the novel, but never detracting from the central narrative thrust; suspense is carefully maintained. Poetic philosophizing, kept under strict control and in moderate dosages, adds a lyrical dimension. The Don Juan motif, seen here as Nature's way of reestablishing order in excessively civilized life, is prominent. The grotesque is objectified in the hydrocephalic infant of the French family with which Ignacio is boarding, as well as in the pathetic rag doll which he keeps in his room after Madame Saint-Julien's death; the doll symbolizes the deceased lover. The character of Ignacio is drawn with a masterly hand and is responsible for much of the keen humor in the novel; at times its humor descends to Rabelaisian crudity, at times rises to sophisticated wit.

L. Zu, el ángel anfibio (Zu, the Amphibious Angel)

Origen, the Alexandrian Christian apologist, in reacting against a popular superstition that whales were the "Devil's fish," went so far as to call them "amphibious angels." Hence the title of Sender's novel, *Zu, el ángel anfibio* (*Zu, the Amphibious Angel*), 1970, a story of a rebel blue whale, Zu, who audaciously questions the ancient and venerated beliefs of whaledom, especially those about men and their life on land. Through his singular viewpoint as a whale, Zu challenges the accepted myth of man's divinity and immortality and spurns the teachings of the "Great Universal Grandfather," a patriarchal, old whale who in Spanish society symbolizes the Catholic Church. In his reasoning against the Church's teachings, including human immortality, Zu simply echoes Marx and Freud, not to mention Communist propaganda.

Through his early discovery of evil done by men, Zu comes to reject the established belief that men are divine. When his beautiful bride, Zetania, dies of suffocation when trapped beneath a cross-Atlantic cable and her body mysteriously disappears, Zu begins an odyssey that finally leads him to death at the hand of whalers. The whole story becomes an allegory of evil and man's (Zu's) undying search for ideal beauty, or for the restoration of a "Lost Paradise." Though not one of Sender's best books, *Zu, the Amphibious Angel* once again reveals the author's great capacity as a storyteller; the book is entertaining and has occasional passages of lyrical force.

M. Tánit (Thanit)

The feminine divinity of Phoenician mythology who was worshipped also by the Carthaginians, Thanit, provides the title for Sender's next novel, *Tánit* (*Thanit*), 1970. A. J. Church believes that Thanit was the primitive name of Astaroth, whose Greek form Astarté has usually been matched with Aphrodite or Venus.[21] While awaiting orders to embark on a dangerous mission to assassinate Sagittarius, the dictator of an unnamed island (veiled allusions to Franco and to Spain), the first-person narrator, Enrique, a thirty-nine-year-old bachelor, by chance meets Thanit, a twenty-three-year-old beauty, whom he recognizes as a girl he knew in Paris seventeen years before (when she was only six); at that earlier time her mother, also named Thanit, and Enrique had been lovers, a fact the daughter never discovers. Enrique and Thanit immediately fall in love and soon decide to be married. Their wedding reception, held in a New York apartment where most of the action, except for an interlude in the Adirondack Mountains, takes place, is attended by such notables as the New England poet Wallace Stevens, Carl Sandburg, Daniel Jones (as the delegate of Dylan Thomas), and others; it provides the author opportunity to expound on poetry, drugs in present-day society, love, death, and literary figures such as Rimbaud, Herbert Read, and Dylan Thomas; the conversations of those present as well as occasional direct musings of his own become the vehicles for expressing what the author has to say in the novel.

Allusions and symbolism in the work are sometimes obscure. The central symbolism, however, is quite certain: Thanit, the young and vital descendant of the ancient goddess, is an incarnation of Enrique's hope for the future of his country; his love for her is his love for Spain, the opposite side of his hate for the tyrant, Sagittarius. Narrative interest is minimal, having been frustrated by the long discussions at the wedding reception and the philosophical musings by Enrique, especially on what he expects to be his impending death. In the end a telegram arrives announcing that Sagittarius has been assassinated by another agent, thus putting an end to Enrique's suspense. A dreamlike atmosphere pervades the entire work; that atmosphere and the passages of poetic force constitute the novel's most positive values. As a whole, *Thanit* is one of the author's least successful novels.

N.   La antesala (The Antechamber)

There are two planes of action in *La antesala* (*The Ante-chamber*), 1971. The present action occurs in Madrid toward the close of the Civil War, one afternoon in which Nazaria, a forty-eight-year-old widow and teacher of retarded children, waits in the hall to see the *comandante* (commander); on this plane the narrative point of view is that of an omniscient author. The central symbolism is obvious: All of life is the antechamber of death. Although momentarily admitted twice into the inner chamber to see the commander, Nazaria is told each time to return to her place in the waiting room before she can conclude her business. Finally tiring of waiting, she wanders out into the street to die from machine gun bullets. "She felt that she was still in the antechamber (the street was an antechamber, also), and she understood that all her life she had been waiting. At times it was a big antechamber, at times not so big, at times with people and at times empty."[22] On the second plane of action, Nazaria reconstructs in her memory (much as Mosén Millán reconstructs the life of Paco in *Requiem for a Spanish Peasant*) the sad and dreary events of her life; she becomes both narrator and protagonist on this second narrative plane. Intermittently Nazaria returns from her musings and memory flashbacks to be conscious of her present surroundings and the voice of the commander in the next room; thus present and past are interwoven into a unity.

Beginning with her bleak childhood and a disease which left her bald, the unattractive Nazaria goes on to recall meeting and later marrying Manuel, a typesetter with a tubercular condition which allowed him only a few years of relative happiness with Nazaria before he expired; the fall of the Monarchy in 1931; Nazaria's private school for mentally retarded children in Madrid, including the grotesque sexual advances made toward her by Juancho, an epileptic with precocious sexual instincts, and the mysterious disappearance of two sisters from the school; the teacher's strange experiences with the false but fantastic "ambassador of Siam," Gustavo; and incidents leading to her decision to seek an audience with the enigmatic *coman-dante*. Integrated into Nazaria's personal story in typically

Senderian fashion are long comments on recent Spanish history, aphoristic musings on the meaning of life and death (reminiscent of *The Sphere*), and at the end a prediction or prophecy by the *comandante* that "the victory that we desire now will succeed" by 1975.[23] *The Antechamber* reveals once again Don Ramón's lasting emotional involvement with the Spanish Civil War.

II   *Historical Novels*

A.   Bizancio (Byzantium)

In 1956 Sender published *Bizancio* (*Byzantium*), the longest of his historical novels and the first of this subgenre to come from his pen since his prizewinning *Mr. Witt Among the Rebels*, twenty years earlier. In the next twelve years he published five more historical novels—the last being *Las criaturas saturnianas* (*The Saturnine Creatures*) in 1968. All seven historical novels are ably analyzed by Francisco Carrasquer in his book, *"Imán" y la novela histórica de Sender* (*"Imán" and Sender's Historical Novels*).[24] In the prologue to Carrasquer's book, Sender writes: ". . . when I wrote *Byzantium* or *Lope de Aguirre* or *The Saturnine Creatures* I added real experiences from my own life with which I enlivened the rigid atmosphere of the past, giving to the events a kind of new or atemporal plasticity and lending force to the characters of the figures of remote yesterday. After all, human nature is the same today as then. Diversity in the use of selective memory is infinite; hence the interest that the world of literary fiction always arouses."[25] Though circumstances differ in the past from those of the present and in Spain from those in Turkey, Sender counts heavily on his knowledge of human psychology to carry his historical novels regardless of the setting or the time. Though relatively faithful to history itself, especially in his recreation of the situation and atmosphere, Sender sacrifices historical detail whenever he deems it required by his novelistic art. An example of historical inexactitude in *Byzantium* is the death of Roger de Flor, commander of the Aragonese mercenary soldiers who went to Constantinople in 1302 to aid the Byzantine King, Andronichus II, in his fight against the Turks, which occurs in Sender's novel as 1303, whereas historians place it in 1306 or 1307. However, as Carrasquer comments, since Sender was not trying "to remake history, but to relive it in his imagination, to novelize it according to the laws of his novelistic universe, the inaccuracies are not important."[26] It did not serve Sender's purposes to keep Roger de Flor alive for more than about the first third of the novel; he is replaced by Berenguer de Rocafort who remains the leader of the expedition until the end of the novel, which coincides with his death in 1309.

Byzantium is a long episodic story of the epic-like adventures and vicissitudes of the Spanish expedition in Turkey during nine bloody years of intrigue, infamous treachery, suffering, and endless battles. One suspects Sender of grossly exaggerating the fabulous victories of the Aragonese. Alborg writes that Sender has in this book "rendered a tribute of passionate admiration for the old heroes of his native land."[27] Sender's primary interest in *Byzantium* is no doubt in the character of the Spaniards, especially the Aragonese, who fought for the Byzantine king. Antonio Tovar, commenting on the book, observes that Sender is preoccupied with the question of Spain, of "what is the essence of that people who sustained a long civil war."[28] It is one of the author's very best historical novels, excelled perhaps only by *Mr. Witt Among the Rebels* and *The Saturnine Creatures.*

B. Los tontos de la Concepción (The Tontos of Conception Mission)

The scene shifts to Arizona in the American Southwest during the eighteenth century in Sender's next historical novel, *Los tontos de la Concepción (The Tontos of Conception Mission),* 1963. This short work (125 pages) was later published as a short story in *El extraño señor Photynos y otras novelas americanas (The Strange Mr. Photynos and Other American Tales),* 1968. *The Tontos of Conception Mission,* subtitled "Missionary Chronicle," is the story, told from the viewpoint of an omniscient author, of two Franciscan priests, Mosén Garcés of Aragon and Father Barraneche, a Navarrese of unchaste habits who impregnates an Indian novitiate; they are on a mission (named

Conception) to the Yuma Indians (the Tontos). Much of the novel's interest derives from the interplay and comparison and contrast between the Spanish priests and their primitive charges, as well as between the moral character of the two priests. An important character is Ginesillo, a Peruvian Indian who as a child had been brought to California by Spaniards and who has since "dropped out" of society, refusing to work. When an associate of his, an Indian who has come to the mission as a spy, escapes from the mission, Ginesillo himself becomes suspect and especially when soon thereafter both Conception and the neighboring mission of Bicuñer are attacked and destroyed as the novel ends.

Sender's long residence in New Mexico and his acquaintance with the sites of old Spanish missions such as Acoma no doubt inspired him to write *The Tontos*. The central personage of the work is Father Garcés, an Aragonese who bears the author's maternal surname; Sender characterizes him with affection and respect as well as with great faithfulness to the mentality of his time, as Carrasquer has observed.[29] In the end Garcés dies heroically as a martyr, tortured more by inner doubts than by outward pain. Taken as a whole the book is not a positive appraisal of Spanish missionary efforts.

C. Carolus Rex (King Charles)

Carolus Rex (*King Charles*), 1963, accurately recreates the atmosphere and circumstances of the Spanish court at a most dismal period in Spanish history, the reign of the last of the Hapsburg dynasty in Spain, Charles II (1665–1700), a sickly monarch sometimes referred to as Charles II the Bewitched (the subtitle of the novel). Perhaps the greatest originality of *King Charles* is its sympathetic and understanding treatment of the much-defamed Spanish king. The author's intention in so portraying Charles II must be explained as one more Senderian effort to achieve in literature a perspective on reality in which ordinary criteria for moral judgments seem to lose their validity.

The novel opens with a second Charles II, the king of England, reading in 1680 a secret report from his ambassador to

Madrid, T. Brown. The report serves merely as a pretext for beginning the narrative which is told by an omniscient author-narrator who announces: "I shall try to reconstruct the facts basing myself on some pages of that secret report, and adding suggestions that occur to me. . . ."[30] The main narrative action begins with preparations for the young monarch's marriage to María Luisa of France, niece of Louis XIV, takes us through the wedding itself, and ends shortly thereafter as the king submits, half-believingly, to the ceremony of exorcism; the story is told in one long stretch, without division into chapters. Court life with its intrigues and fierce ambitions (especially those of Don Juan José of Austria), scandal and pettiness, provides the vivid but decadent atmosphere and background for the personal adventures of the ill-starred Spanish monarch. Humor, especially as related to the king's sexual desires, is crude.

For its imaginative yet realistic portrayal of a significant though unfortunate period in Spain's history, and its originality in characterizing the "Imbecile King" of Spain, *King Charles* is noteworthy; it is not, however, one of the author's better novels.

D. La aventura equinocial [*sic*] de Lope de Aguirre (The Equinoctial Adventure of Lope de Aguirre)

The Basque, Lope de Aguirre, "the traitor" and "madman," becomes the protagonist of Sender's next historical novel, *La aventura equinocial* [*sic*] *de Lope de Aguirre* (*The Equinoctial Adventure of Lope de Aguirre*), 1964, which relates the Spanish expedition down the Amazon River to its mouth and around the Venezuelan coast to Barquisimeto, Venezuela, from September, 1560, until October, 1561. The characterization of Lope de Aguirre, a hardened and embittered veteran of the Spanish conquest of Peru suffering from paranoia and a demented thirst for power, is masterfully executed and maintained throughout this second longest of Sender's historical novels; indeed the creation of Lope de Aguirre is the work's chief literary merit.

Aguirre joins the expedition of Captain Pedro de Ursúa to seek for a fabled city of fantastic wealth, *El Dorado,* and is assigned the lowly office of *tenedor de difuntos,* "keeper of the

dead." Immediately he begins to scheme to usurp control of
the expedition. "This is the topsy-turvy time in which some
men rise from nothing to the top: Pizarro, Almagro, Cortés,
De Soto."[31] In northern Peru he had become known as "Aguirre
the madman"; it was precisely his "madness" and radical rebellion against all authority, earthly or divine, which enabled him
to make his way by intrigue and murder to the place of almost
absolute power over the expeditionaries (who numbered 240
Spaniards, fifty-five Indians, and twenty Negroes when they finally
reached the mouth of the Amazon). Having assumed command,
Aguirre proclaims his famous twenty *reniegos,* all violent denials
of or blasphemies against the King of Spain, Philip II, and his
own name as a Spaniard.

As the expedition descends the Amazon, Aguirre terrorizes
his men by ordering more and more executions, often on the
mere suspicion of subversion or because he regarded the victims
as useless or "undesirable." His deeds assume epic propórtions,
but in a negative, destructive sense. Upon landing on the Venezuelan coast near Barquisimeto, Aguirre's forces encounter Spanish troops under the command of García de Paredes; when
the majority of his men desert to Paredes, Aguirre is left in a
hopeless situation. Before surrendering and being killed by a
Spanish soldier, he slays his beautiful fourteen-year-old daughter, Elvira (symbol of his transcendent ideal), to prevent her
being known as the "daughter of the traitor" and being violated
by unworthy men.[32] Aguirre's dead body is quartered, placed
in a cage, and displayed publicly.

Powerful psychological realism, well-documented story and
recreation of atmosphere, vigorous dialogue, direct and verbal
style, grim humor, lively vignettes of historical figures (Ursúa,
Pedrarias, Orellana, Guzmán, etc.), and other standard Senderian
qualities make *Lope de Aguirre* a worthwhile novel. Yet the
work suffers from excessive repetitiousness in theme and episode;
reduced to half its present length, it could have gained
artistically.

E.   Tres novelas teresianas (Three Theresan Novels)

As pointed out in my discussion of *The Word Became Sex*
(*Theresa of Jesus*) in Chapter 3, Sender wrote *Tres novelas*

teresianas (*Three Theresan Novels*), 1967, to replace the earlier, immature novel which he has called a "sin" of his childhood. Although containing some material found in *The Word Became Sex*, essentially his later work, *Three Theresan Novels*, is a new book; we have, therefore, two novels expressive of Sender's lifelong interest in the Saint of Avila, one published in 1931 (but composed much earlier) and the other appearing in 1967. The primary thesis of the earlier work—that the Saint was truly possessed by love—remains unchanged in the later novel. Both works are also alike in their implied protest against the socio-political abuses of the sixteenth century, clearly an indirect reflection upon the contemporary Spanish scene.

Each of the three *novelas* (tales or novelettes, in this case) can be read as a separate story. Yet there is such unity and continuity among them that they may more appropriately be regarded as three parts or chapters of a single novel. Each part focuses on a crucial moment in Theresa's life; the Saint moves against the rich historical background of her day imaginatively recreated by the author. Metaphysical speculation, a Senderian constant, is not excessive.

Sender portrays Theresa with sympathy and intuitive understanding. Her saintliness is a manifestation of *hombría*, that mysterious source of holiness, heroism, and poetry. Her consuming love made it impossible for her to judge harshly any man, including the monstrously egoistic King Philip II. Reality and fantasy mingle in typically Senderian fashion. Don Quixote and Sancho Panza chat with Theresa while attending a miracle play, "The House of Lot," integrated into the first *novela;* Don Juan pays a nocturnal (and anachronistic) visit to Princess Ana de Éboli's bedroom; and Lazarillo de Tormes tricks the Saint out of a few coppers. The book is an interesting and unique addition to the extensive Theresan bibliography.

F.   Las criaturas saturnianas (The Saturnine Creatures)

Sender's last historical novel *Las criaturas saturnianas* (*The Saturnine Creatures*), 1968, derives a certain unity from its protagonist, Princess Tarakanova, niece of Catherine the Great of Russia late in the eighteenth century. It follows her fortunes

during her exile as an adolescent in Florence, her return as a
young woman to Russia to suffer inhumanly in prison for over
a decade in St. Petersburg, her release and subsequent journey-
ing across Europe to Florence. En route to Italy she is joined
in Central Europe by Cagliostro, a fraudulent count, adventurer,
and practitioner of the occult. Effervescent with life although
advanced in years, Cagliostro becomes the leading though by
no means exclusive vehicle for the articulation of Sender's unique
vision of life and reality. The count accompanies the princess
during the rest of the novel, talking endlessly and taking her
on a detour to northern Spain. The Spanish "detour," which
occupies two-fifths of the book's length, is of central importance.

In Spain the princess and the count witness an *aquelarre,* a
witches' Sabbath, described in an earlier novel by Sender,
Emen hetan (*Here We Are*), 1958; the earlier novel is here
incorporated into *The Saturnine Creatures.* At the witches'
Sabbath Princess Tarakanova meets the third principal character in the narrative, Spic, a madman who slays his three-year-
old son in homage to Satan. (Thus he, as does the title of the
novel itself, symbolizes modern man who sacrifices his sons to
dark, irrational forces. Saturn, as the Greek god, Cronus, was
known in Italy, swallowed his children as soon as they were
born.) Spic holds a position antithetical to that of Cagliostro
whose magic is white, i.e., affirmative rather than negative or
purely destructive. The long verbal interchanges between these
two strange personages, oscillating between the ridiculous and
the sublime, carry much of the work's philosophical-religious
import. Indifferent to their discourses yet attentive is the princess
whom extreme suffering has driven to the margin of life, making
her a silent, passive figure with a perspective on reality that
sees above good and evil, joy and sorrow, even life and death.
As such she incarnates the author's theory of reality as neither
bad nor good, most notably expressed in *The Sphere.* "Evil" is
only a necessary part of "good," darkness of light, etc. Excessive
somberness is avoided by Sender's superb humor in dialogue
and situation.

The simple and unaffected style ranges from brutal realism
(the subhuman experiences of the princess in prison) to highly
lyrical passages (adventures and personages in the castle in

Spain). The novel is at its poetic best in the chapters which relate the time spent by the count and the princess in Spic's ancient castle, high in the Pyrenees near the French border. Defects include needless and excessively long digressions as well as repetitious harping on certain points or themes. Unless the reader is unusually well-read in the history of ancient religions, he may be bewildered by some obscure references in *The Saturnine Creatures*.

CHAPTER 8

Other Genres

SENDER reminds one of members of the Generation of Eighteen Ninety-Eight, especially of Unamuno, in his deliberate blurring of the boundaries established between genres established by critics. Senderian "plays" have later been published as "short stories," "novels" as "short stories"; expository and narrative prose are inextricably united in such books as *Tres ejemplos de amor y una teoría* (*Three Examples of Love and a Theory*), and *Relatos fronterizos* (*Frontier Reports*), a miscellaneous collection of seventeen "reports" consisting of anecdotes, narrative-essays, essays, and general commentary. Though Don Ramón excels as a writer of fiction, primarily as a novelist but also as a writer of short stories, his work in the theater, poetry, essay, and journalism is meritorious and substantial. His early, intense work as a journalist, especially as an editor of the Madrilian newspaper, *El Sol*, was of decisive importance in his formation as a writer. In his own words, his experience with *El Sol* gave him "a certain ease of expression," and taught him how to write "only interesting things. That is, not to be boring."[1] Sender's concern is not with genre but with expressing himself in a way that will interest the reader. It should be clear that my classification of certain books in this chapter may be more a matter of convenience than of strict accuracy (especially, for example, in the case of the two books mentioned above).

I Short Stories

A. Mexicayotl

In 1940 Sender published his first book of short stories, *Mexicayotl* (Nahuatl for "Song of Mexico"), a collection of nine

148

tales of Mexican life. In the preface to the book, the author asserts that he had been inspired to write the stories from his reading of the works of the sixteenth-century writer Friar Bernardino de Sahagún and from his recent travels in Mexico. They are, he writes, a definition of "the virgin Mexican nature as I feel it."[2] In all the narratives in which fantasy has free rein, Sender has shown an unusually keen sensitivity to nature and especially to animal life; the book is valuable for its humor and poetic symbolism as well as for its sympathetic and penetrating portrayal of the Mexican Indian.

B.   Novelas ejemplares de Cíbola (Exemplary Tales of Cibola)

Twenty-one years after the appearance of *Mexicayotl*, Sender published his second volume of short stories, *Novelas ejemplares de Cíbola* (*Exemplary Tales of Cibola*), 1961. Five of its twelve stories are taken directly, and a sixth in revised form, from *Mexicayotl*; the remaining six narratives are set in the Southwest (Cibola) and vividly reflect the local color and flavor of that region's rich racial and cultural mixtures. They are: "Professor St. John Comes of Age," "Father Zozobra," "The Terrace," "Adventure in Bethany," "Delgadina," and "Desert Guests." These last, especially "Father Zozobra," "The Terrace," and "Desert Guests," are undoubtedly among Sender's very finest stories.

Space here does not permit adequate consideration of the excellent narratives in *Exemplary Tales of Cibola*. An example of Sender at his very best is "Father Zozobra," a deeply sensitive portrayal of an alcoholic Spanish priest in a monastery which served as a kind of rehabilitation home for wayward Catholic clerics in New Mexico. Father Zozobra, whose name means worry, anguish, gloom, is a man in his fifties who was expelled from his Castilian village-parish for having carnal relations with his young housekeeper, and who has subsequently wandered from the Philippines to Borneo to California; finally he has been sent to the correctional institution in New Mexico. He is able to reconcile himself to his role as a priest in the Church's hierarchy only while in an alcoholic stupor; through Zozobra's memory-flashbacks and interior monologue, his delicate interactions on the present time-level with the local barkeeper and his wife and especially with Malinche, an attractive young Indian woman, and her fiancé, Bernardo, Sender has with depth and compassion created one of his most memorable characters.

Father Zozobra suffered because he could not adapt himself to institutionalized religion which seemed to deny the very spirit of Jesus Christ. He dared to say to the abbot that the "day the Pope works like any laborer to earn his living, the Church will have greater authority.... Let us imagine the Pope working in a carpenter's shop..."[3] The author-narrator intervenes: "There were no solutions on earth and the bishops offered solutions. This was what Father Zozobra could not endure—the bishops offering solutions in exchange for the silver cigarette holder and gold-embroidered slippers. There were no solutions on earth, save Calvary..."[4] To the priest it seemed that the Church was a commercial enterprise which sold solutions for money.

A beautiful and moving parallel is made in "Father Zozobra" between man and the century plant which supposedly blooms only in its hundredth Spring, just before dying. " 'Why shouldn't we men also humbly give our blossom and die?' " asks the priest as he admires the plant. " 'The life of a man, however vulgar and despicable, has its value. More or less important, that value ties in with the whole of creation and adds something to it. Something that creation did not have before.' "[5] It is hard to find a more beautiful statement of Sender's faith in life.

C. Tales of Cibola

Seven stories from *Novelas ejemplares de Cíbola* (*Exemplary Tales of Cíbola*), in addition to two new pieces, "The Tonatiu" and "The Red Light," make up Sender's only book of short stories in English translation, *Tales of Cibola*, 1964.

The scene for "The Tonatiu" is Mexico City. Based on the Mexican legend of the Tonatiu, the sun god who descends in disguise to walk among men on cloudy days, the story is another example of the author's interest in mythology. For the most part "The Tonatiu" consists of humorous but serious semiphilosophical, semireligious exchanges between the author-narrator (who is mistakenly known as Ramírez) and Photynos, a weird

Mexican of Greek origin who suggests that he himself is the sun god or his delegate, the brother of Christ, Dionysius, and Black Trinidad of Sender's novel, *Dark Wedding.*

"The Red Light" is the ironic story, told by old Jelinek, tavern-keeper in an American industrial city, of a rich prostitute who had herself buried in a costly mausoleum. Right after her death the city installed a red traffic light at the street corner bordering her tomb.

D. Cabrerizas Altas

Sender's next volume of short stories, *Cabrerizas Altas* (a town in Spanish Morocco), takes its title from the first of its three stories; "Cabrerizas Altas" is a brilliantly executed, rather long short story (eighty-five pages in the book). Its narrator-protagonist, Alfonso, a corporal in an infantry disciplinary regiment in Melilla during the Moroccan campaign, falls in love with a tavern waitress in the bleak little town of Cabrerizas Altas. Alfonso's unsuccessful attempts to fulfill his passionate devotion to a waitress of unknown origin is an allegory of man's pursuit of the ideal or beauty, the theme of Don Quixote and Dulcinea. The story end with the ideal still unrealized but the corporal, battered and bruised, refuses to renounce his quest. "My life is not finished, not by a long shot," he meditates while recuperating in a French hospital. "It could still begin."[6] Meanwhile the girl lives in a squalid desert hut as the mistress of a renegade Spaniard, the man whom she had regarded as her father until a recent blood test proved otherwise.

The second story in the volume *Cabrerizas Altas*, "El Tonatiu," formerly appeared in English in *Tales of Cibola*, and has already been discussed. The last story is "Las rosas de Pasadena" ("The Roses of Pasadena"), which relates the strange reactions of seven inmates of death row in San Quentin prison (including Caryl Chessman) when they gather to watch on television the Pasadena Rose Parade.

E. La llave y otras narraciones (The Key and Other Narrations)

The title story for Sender's collection of five short stories, *The Key and Other Narrations*, 1967,[7] was originally staged as a one-act play of three scenes in the Spanish Theater of Madrid in 1936.[8] Its English translation, "The Key," was published later in *The Kenyon Review* (Winter 1943), and in 1945 it was staged in New York City under the auspices of the art journal, *View— The Modern Magazine*.[9] Substantially the story is the same as the play.

When Rosenda refuses to return to her miser husband, Avelino, the key to his treasure chest, "a cute little key with its little letters, and its tiny hole for the little mouse,"[10] she would have been strangled to death had her daughter by a former marriage not appeared on the scene in time to beat the old man unconscious with a bottle. As Avelino lies unconscious, Fau, the old man's illegitimate and feeble-minded son, having just discovered the treasure chest hidden in a shed, appears and demands the key; Rosenda tells him that his father, before dying of a stroke, had swallowed it; the story ends as Fau rips open his father's stomach to find the key. Rosenda, by tricking Fau into thinking that his father was dead (and thus encouraging him to cut Avelino open in his greedy search for the key), has assured that Fau will go to prison for his crime while she, secure in the possession of the key, will enjoy freedom and riches. Man's savage greed and capacity for demonic cruelty are evident themes here. The action occurs in a nightmarish atmosphere.

Of the same morally grotesque character as "The Key" are the next two stories in the book: "Doctor Velasco's Daughter," and "The Anniversary Photograph." In the first story, in order to protect the reputation of his dead daughter whom he idealizes as an embodiment of virginal purity, Doctor Velasco falsely declares permanently insane an old aristocrat so that his greedy relatives may obtain their inheritance. In the second story, which was originally published as a one-act play,[11] Teodosio, a photographer, on his silver wedding anniversary learns that his wife, Rosario, is to have her first baby. A dark suspicion enters his mind: Recently Rosario has associated rather closely with an irresponsible loafer, Gustavo, who a few nights before fell into the water and drowned while drunk and walking along a dike with Rosario. Had Rosario pushed him into the water? In the end Teodosio philosophically accepts his own impotence and his wife's defections, and joins Rosario in joyful anticipation of the "blessed event."

In "El pelagatos y la flor de nieve" ("The Poor Wretch and the Snow Flower"), the fourth story, Iván Garcidueñas, an American high school teacher, is beset with remorse and doubt after having chloroformed his old cat, and begun its vivisection for the benefit of his students. Panic ensues among the students when the skinned cat seems to come alive. Three weeks later the cat (Or a similar one? Or a figment of Iván's inflamed imagination?) appears to Iván on a snowy day at the airport where he waits in vain for his fiancée to meet him; they were to fly to another city and be married. A "flower" of crystallized snow on the airport window comes to symbolize beauty or the ideal "much anterior to the existence of any kind of protoplasm."[12]

The last piece in the collection, "Mary-Lou," is a tender story of the author's relations with Mary-Lou, an eight-year-old girl who visited him daily in the park during his vacation in San Diego. An old man who strips to his shorts every day and harangues the people in the park with gloomy prophetic quotations from the Bible provides a touch of grotesque humor.

F. Las gallinas de Cervantes (Cervantes' Hens)

Las gallinas de Cervantes y otras narraciones parabólicas (*Cervantes' Hens and Other Parabolic Stories*), 1967, consists of four allegorical stories: "Las gallinas de Cervantes" ("Cervantes' Hens"), "El sosia y los delegados" ("The Double and the Delegates"), "Parábola de Jesús y el inquisidor" ("Allegory of Jesus and the Inquisitor"), and "Aventura del Angelus I" ("Adventure of Angelus I").

"Cervantes' Hens" is a surrealistic tale of the progressive and grotesque transformation of Cervantes' wife into a hen-woman, who "sleeps" perched on the crossbars at the head of her husband's bed. There are stories within a story, occasional humor to relieve the oppressive atmosphere, and nightmarish scenes reminiscent of Kafka's *Metamorphosis*. It seems that the author wishes to represent the growing dehumanization of society. Balancing this bleak outlook is the humanity of Cervantes and the everpresent "faith" or idealism of Sender, expressed here in esoteric references to Dulcinea, "the sweet lady of the secret goodness,"[13] and in the hidden nobility of Don Alonso, uncle to Cervantes' wife.

"The Double" tells of what happened when Stalin's double (*el sosia*) suddenly presents himself, three years after the death of the Russian dictator, in a Congress of Soviet delegates with the announcement that he is Stalin—an interesting narrative with a political lesson for men desiring to remain free. "Allegory of Jesus and the Inquisitor" is an adaptation of a chapter from *The Brothers Karamazov* by Dostoevski, and relates the visit of Jesus to Seville and his long conversation with Torquemada, the Inquisitor. As with the Hebraic religious organization, so Jesus now finds himself at odds with the Catholic Church.

In "Adventure of Angelus I," Sender as narrator-author-protagonist visits Mars and Jupiter in a spaceship. His dialogue with a Martian becomes the medium for the author's most ambitious striving after an apprehension of total reality and brings to mind his metaphysical-religious probing in *The Sphere*. Jupiter turns out to be occupied by giant cockroaches and symbolizes the fate that awaits the Earth if men continue their march toward a nuclear holocaust. He calls for a synthesis between reason and vital instinct (represented by man's ganglia), a synthesis which appears to be similar or parallel to the *razón vital* advocated by Ortega y Gasset in *The Theme of Our Time*.

G. El extraño señor Photynos (The Strange Mr. Photynos)

Don Ramón's next book of short stories, *El extraño señor Photynos y otras novelas americanas* (*The Strange Mr. Photynos and Other American Tales*), 1968, contains five *novelas*, all with American settings: "The Strange Mr. Photynos" ("The Tonatiu" with a new and more enticing title), "The Tontos of Conception Mission" (discussed in Chapter 7 as a historical novel), "The Friend Who Bought a Picasso," "The Red Light," and "The Roses of Pasadena." The only new work in the collection not already discussed is "The Friend Who Bought a Picasso," in which the author-narrator and his wife, Margaret, are dinner guests in the home of Bryan, a retired businessman, and his spouse, Charlotte, who are having marital difficulties. Inspired by a Picasso painting which Bryan had acquired a few years earlier, the author-narrator relates his strange love affair with a Spanish beauty.

H. Novelas del otro jueves (Tales of the Other Thursday)

Four of the seven narratives in *Tales of the Other Thursday*, 1969 ("Cervantes' Hens," "The Double and the Delegates," "Jesus and the Inquisitor," and "Adventure of Angelus I") are reprinted from an earlier book, *Cervantes' Hens and Other Parabolic Stories*; the three new stories are "Edelmiro's Return," "The Urucurú," and "The Viaduct." The first relates the brutal humiliation and disillusionment awaiting middle-aged Edelmiro when, after an absence of twenty-nine years in America, he returns in happy anticipation to his native Spanish village. In "The Urucurú," the second new story, El Choto, head of an Indian family on an island in a Venezuelan lake, apprehensively hides his beautiful daughter, Dominica (symbol of purity?), when Humboldt, the German naturalist, visits the island in search of a rare species of wild duck, the *urucurú*. "The Viaduct" is set in Madrid during the Civil War. When a prostitute comes to the viaduct intent on committing suicide Andrés, a policeman who is there to stop her, converses with her and becomes so intrigued that he follows her in her plunge to death.

I. Relatos fronterizos (Frontier Reports)

A diverse collection of seventeen "reports" (anecdotes, narrative-essays, commentary, and essays), *Relatos fronterizos* (*Frontier Reports*), 1970, gains a sense of unity not only from its common reflection of Sender's distinctive viewpoint and personal experiences, but also from its focus on a single theme: the "frontiers" between different cultures and ways of perceiving the world; thus the French artist Utrillo, the North American criminal Chessman, and the translator of Sender's first novel into German, Neuendorf, are "frontier" characters. Along with anecdotal discussions of individuals there are *relatos* which both narrate and reflect on the author's personal experiences in such different places as London, Acapulco, the Grand Canyon, Paris, El Paso, and Moscow. In one "report," the "black panthers" of the United States are discussed; in another the author relates his personal witnessing of discrimination against Mexicans in Texas; in another the strange story of Don Gaspar, a half-Spanish Catholic priest in Peru, who learned to play the *quena* (Indian

flute) recalls the *tradiciones peruanas* (Peruvian traditions) of
Ricardo Palma; etc.

Other short stories by Sender not appearing in the books
briefly considered in the foregoing section have appeared occasionally in anthologies and periodicals.[14]

II *Theatre*

Spanish writers, sooner or later, seem to have a propensity
for the theater and for playwriting. Even Cervantes, Galdós,
Unamuno, Azorín, and Baroja—to mention only some of the
greatest writers who were not primarily dramatists—wrote theater.
Sender has hardly been an exception. Though not published,
one of his earliest plays in the 1930's, *El Cristo* (*The Christ*),
was adapted cinematically. Unfortunately, both manuscript and
film were lost during the Civil War. Two other Senderian plays,
El sumario (*The Summary*) and *El duelo* (*The Duel*), also
disappeared during that conflict. Though neither had been published, both had been enacted on the stage.[15]

A. El secreto (The Secret)

Certainly one of Sender's most moving dramatic works, perhaps his very best, is *El secreto* (*The Secret*), a one-act play
published in Madrid in 1935.[16] Its scene is set in Barcelona in the
office of the Chief of Police on the eve of a scheduled revolution.
Through torture the police are seeking to obtain from two
political prisoners "the secret": the plans of the revolutionaries.
Seeing that his companion is about to reveal the plans, the second
prisoner promises to give the desired information in exchange
for the execution of his companion. Once the execution is completed, the surviving prisoner, knowing that he alone knows the
"secret," invites the police to shoot him as the lights in the city
go out—the signal for the beginning of the uprising.

B. Hernán Cortés

Sender's first book-length theatrical work, *Hernán Cortés*,
1940, has never been staged. In the "Noticia" ("Notice") at the

beginning of the book, Sender wrote: "As the readers will see it is a little *retablo* [series of historical scenes]. Those who are fond of history and of the theater will doubtlessly enjoy it—as I enjoyed writing it."[17] The work might more accurately be classified as a *novela dialogada* (dialogued novel) as James O. Swain has suggested.[18] Divided into two parts and eleven scenes with a wide diversity in place and time, it is not surprising that the work has never been staged. Perhaps its greatest value is its superb characterization of Cortés, accomplished almost exclusively through dialogue. Typically Senderian is the emphasis in *Hernán Cortés* upon human dignity and heroism. Realistic and fantastic planes frequently intersect.

C. "The House of Lot"

Sender's interest in the Old Testament is seen in his short, one-act play, "The House of Lot," which has been published only in English and German.[19] In this play which resembles the Spanish religious plays known as *autos sacramentales* in the Middle Ages, Sender has derived his own original meaning from the biblical narrative, freely expanding its nucleus to accommodate his own interpretation. Characterization of Lot, the righteous man, is well done. The play appears in Sender's novel, *Three Theresan Novels*, integrated into the narrative framework of the first of the three "novels"; Don Quixote and Sancho Panza are spectators in the audience as it is staged.

D. El diantre (The Devil)

Sender's continuing interest in evil is seen in *El diantre* (*The Devil*), 1958, a play in seven acts which bears the subtitle: "Tragic-comedy for the Screen According to a Story by [the Russian writer Leonidas] Andreiev." It was later reworked into six acts and given the longer title of "Comedia del diantre" ("Comedy of the Devil") for its second edition.[20] Following the tradition of the classic Spanish theater, its personages symbolize moral values. When the millionaire Charles Reinhardt dies, the Devil incarnates himself in his body, and is thus enabled to sustain a prolonged conversation with Logus, a scientist who is seeking the secret formula to destroy the universe. Beside the wiles and evil of men the Devil appears to be a mere amateur. Noteworthy is *The Devil's* racy dialogue and typical Senderian humor, a humor which gives some relief from its disturbingly dark view of human evil.

E. "The Wind"

In 1963 Don Ramón published in English "The Wind,"[21] a one-act morality play which portrays a fifty-year-old Protestant pastor who is convinced that God has told him to kill his son, a thirty-year-old cripple. Alone in their isolated home overlooking the ocean, father and son desperately talk about impending death while, outside, the wind, symbolic of dark fatalistic forces, moans and shrieks. The timely appearance of Pamela, symbol of ideal love, in the end saves the son.

F. Jubileo en el Zócalo (Jubilee in the Zócalo)

Inspired by reading *The Bernal Díaz Chronicles*, the famous account of the Spanish conquest of Mexico by a soldier in the ranks of Hernando Cortés, Bernal Díaz del Castillo, Sender wrote especially as a reader for college students of Spanish *Jubileo en el Zócalo (Jubilee in the Zócalo)*, 1964; he reworked it slightly for its definitive edition published in 1967. Set within a narrative framework (which is mostly dialogue and, therefore, capable of theatrical representation) is a *retablo* or series of dramatic historical pictures; the "jubilee" occurs in Mexico City's main square, the Zócalo, in 1538, in celebration of a peace agreement that year between Spain and France. In a series of scenes the Spanish conquest of Mexico, essentially concluded fifteen years earlier, is reenacted while Spanish participants in that conquest, Cortés, Alvarado, Father Bartolomé, Bernal Díaz del Castillo, and others are most interested spectators. There is lively interaction between these survivors in the audience and those playing the parts of those who died in that epic struggle. Though Cortés emerges as a hero, albeit a very human one, Sender's evident disdain for two Spanish leaders, Governor Diego Velázquez and Captain Pánfilo de Narváez, and his great admiration for the Indians lend balance to the total work.

G. Don Juan en la mancebía (Don Juan in the Brothel)

In addition to Don Quixote, Spain has given Don Juan to the world. It is not surprising that Sender's next drama, *Don Juan en la mancebía* (*Don Juan in the Brothel*), 1968, should deal with this enigmatic figure. On the eve of All Saints' Day in 1635 in Seville, Don Juan, now seventy years of age, visits a bawdy-house where he and Beatriz, a twenty-four-year-old prostitute, are mutually attracted to one another. Incest is averted when Don Juan discovers that Beatriz is his daughter, conceived on the night of his violation of Doña Inés. Father and daughter then visit the pantheon which Don Juan has had constructed for himself in the cemetery; there the old libertine is killed by Miguel de Mañara, probably out of jealousy over Don Juan's reputation. Don Juan then joins Doña Inés in the invisible world from which he continues to talk and act in the play (just as Inés does from the beginning); from the antechamber of eternity (Heaven or Hell?), Juan and Inés are indignant but impotent as they observe and protest the summary execution of their daughter, Beatriz, by the Spanish Inquisition (in order to obtain the inheritance left her by her father). Sender's continuing struggle to define the nature of evil is evident in his fantastic yet faithful interpretation of Don Juan whose final essence remains as inexplicable as does evil itself. Beautiful passages of poetic speculations about death, and humorous and ingenious dialogue lift this work above the ordinary; although it makes excellent reading, it could also be very effectively staged.

H. Comedia del diantre y otras dos (Play of the Devil and Two Others)

The first play in *Play of the Devil and Two Others*, 1969, has already been discussed under its first and shorter title, *The Devil*. The first of the new works here discussed is obscurely entitled, "Los antofagastas," which could be translated as "The Anthophagous Creatures." Anthophagous insects live by feeding on flowers, and the title doubtlessly refers to the three male scientists in the play who, though claiming to be above passion, quarrel over Priscilla whose physical love they have all known. The setting is in the Amazonian jungle where the scientists have been sent to measure radiation from a nuclear explosion; the time is the present era. In the end a figure representing death lands in a helicopter to take one scientist, Bob, and Priscilla (who is bald beneath her wig) to an unknown destiny, leaving Conrad and Arístides alone in the jungle. Subtitled "Mystery in Three Acts," the play is overladen with allusions and references of a lyric but esoteric nature; all in all, as drama it is an unsuccessful experiment.

The setting for "Donde crece la marihuana [sic]" ("Where the Marijuana Grows"),[22] a play in four acts, is on a ranch in Arizona in contemporary times; the problem posed is that of the "impertinent curious one," a story intercalated in Don Quixote. One of Sender's more representable plays, its recreation of the colorful Southwestern atmosphere and poetic commentary on the problem of the "impertinent curious one" are noteworthy.

III Poetry

No matter what his medium, Sender always strives for the poetic effect. In his long book of poetry, dedicated "To the children of my compatriots, born in exile," Las imágenes migratorias (The Migratory Images), 1960, Don Ramón expresses the same Weltanschauung already known to readers of his prose. Seventeen of the book's seventy-eight poems are gozos or glees to the Dame of Elche, symbol of ideal feminine virginity, frequently alluded to in Sender's novels. The poems focus on man and his relation to the cosmos and to the temporal society in which he lives, although these two dimensions (the metaphysical and the social) constitute a unified view in Sender's private world and are, therefore, distinguishable but hardly separable. It is impossible here to do more than to mark the existence of The Migratory Images; in a short, appreciative study of its poetry, Rafael Bosch ably summarizes the poet's philosophical positions as follows: "Life is not only our creation, our responsibility, the result of our choice, in the manner popularized by Sartre, but an elemental force making us become what we are. And this reality more powerful than our determination is not only life in a biological sense, but the meaning of spiritual vitality."[23]

IV *Journalistic Works and Essays*

Sender's journalistic works and books of essays will be briefly examined here in the order of their publication dates.

A. Journalistic Works

Don Ramón's first book, *El problema religioso en Méjico* (*The Religious Problem in Mexico*), 1928, appeared when Mexico was seething with Catholic opposition to separation of Church and State; its contents are based primarily on articles which had previously appeared in *El Sol*. A well-written, vigorous attack upon the political and moral corruption of the Catholic Church during its history in Mexico, the book tries to show that the Mexican State, a secular institution, has shown more of the spirit of Christ than has the Church itself; it is significant that its subtitle is *Catholics and Christians*.

In 1930 Sender collected articles which had formerly appeared in the newspaper, *La Libertad*, and published them in a 65-page booklet entitled *América antes de Colón* (*America Before Columbus*), announced as the first of a series of three booklets on the history of America. Sender discusses several Indian groups, especially the Aztecs and the Mayas, and ends with a chapter sharply critical of the role of the Catholic Church in the Spanish Conquest and afterwards.

Teatro de masas (*People's Theater*), 1932, is a collection of thirteen brief chapters which formerly had appeared as articles in *La Libertad* of Madrid. In it Sender argues eloquently for the creation of a theater in Spain that would appeal to the masses and would express the most vital realities of the Spanish scene.

As a free-lance reporter Sender visited Casas Viejas, an Andalusian village in which an uprising of peasants (January 9–12, 1933) had been brutally repressed by the Spanish Government. His reports appeared as articles in *La Libertad*, and were later hastily compiled to form *Casas Viejas*, a volume of 103 pages published later the same year; its contents are the basis for the novel, *Trip to the Village of Crime*, published the following year.

As a guest of the International Union of Writers Sender, the successful young novelist and journalist with strong Communistic leanings, attended the Olympiad of Revolutionary Art in Moscow in May of 1933 and remained in the Soviet Union for about two months. As a living document of the reactions of a Spanish idealist to the Soviet system during a period of world-wide economic depression, Sender's book of impressions of his visit, *Madrid–Moscú* (*Madrid–Moscow*), 1934, is interesting and valuable. It is by no means uncritical of the Soviet scene. "I know that the Communists are not going to like what I am going to say," Sender asserts, "but I am not writing for them, but for myself and to give my readers a complete and truthful impression."[24] To a surprising degree the book impresses with its objectivity.

The title of Sender's next book of essays, *Carta de Moscú sobre el amor* (*Letter from Moscow on Love*), 1934, is somewhat misleading inasmuch as it is basically a criticism of sexual relations and prejudices in Spain rather than a report on the amorous relationship in Russia; Sender attacks the Spanish tendency to think of matter (sex) as evil and spirit as good, and argues for a more wholesome acceptance of one's sexuality. The main points of the book are restated in the last chapter of Sender's book, *Tres ejemplos de amor y una teoría* (*Three Examples of Love and a Theory*) in 1969.

Proclamación de la sonrisa (*Proclamation of the Smile*), another of five Senderian volumes published in 1934, consists of fifty-eight short chapters or compositions on themes of the most diversified nature; almost exclusively they are commentary on political, social, and literary issues of the day. Sender's terse and vigorous style as well as his distinct views makes *Proclamation* a noteworthy book; many, if not all, of its chapters had formerly appeared in *La Libertad*.

Crónica del pueblo en armas (*Chronicle of the People in Arms*) is a forty-six page propagandistic pamphlet (published under the auspices of the Fifth Regiment of the Spanish Loyalist Forces early in the Civil War in 1936) which seeks to relate the historical struggle of the Spanish masses against the Monarchy and the Church to the conflict then underway.

Contraataque appeared in English translation in both the United States (as *Counter-Attack in Spain*) and in England

(as *The War in Spain*) in 1937, one year before its publication
in Barcelona in Spanish. Leland Stowe has called it "the simple
record of what one man experienced, saw and felt during the
first six months of Franco's war."[25] Essentially it is a personal
narrative of the author's experiences and observations as an
active combatant with the Loyalist forces.

B. Essays

Sender's most controversial book of essays is his volume,
Unamuno, Valle-Inclán, Baroja y Santayana, which he published in 1955 during his eighth year as professor of Spanish
literature at the University of New Mexico. Three of the book's
four essays are on distinguished members of the Spanish Generation of 1898; the fourth discusses the well-known Harvard
professor and author, George Santayana. Though Santayana
wrote all his work in English, Sender claims that he "may be
considered a Hispanic writer, including one of the Generation
of 1898."[26] Sender personally knew the first three authors, although his acquaintance with Baroja was very slight. The first
essay is a violent and subjective attack upon both Unamuno
the man and the artist, and constitutes a kind of "minority report" on a man almost universally admired by all who know his
work.[27] Baroja and his work are brilliantly analyzed although
not with the generous disposition to understand and appreciate
that is evident in Sender's examination of his close personal
friend, Ramón del Valle-Inclán. The section on Santayana is
a masterful portrayal of the author of *The Last Puritan* as essentially a Spanish writer (though the Harvard philosopher left
Spain as a child in 1872 never to return, and did not speak
Spanish). These essays, impregnated with Sender's own distinctive and personal vision, are filled with illuminating insights
into Spanish character, life, and art; though unscientific in
approach and character, they are eminently readable. Sender
reworked his essays on Unamuno, Baroja, and Santayana, reprinted the essay on Valle-Inclán, and added three chapters
(one each on Azorín, Ramiro de Maeztu, and Juan Ramón
Jiménez) for *Examen de ingenios; los noventayochos* (*Examination of Talents; Those of 1898*), 1961, which may be regarded

as an augmented and revised second edition of *Unamuno, Valle-Inclán, Baroja y Santayana*.

Don Ramón's high esteem for Valle-Inclán is further seen in his long essay published as a book in Spain in 1965: *Valle-Inclán y la dificultad de la tragedia* (*Valle-Inclán and the Difficulty of Tragedy*). The shorter essay in *Unamuno, Valle-Inclán, Baroja y Santayana* is in the new book augmented to include a discussion of the totality of the Galician author's works, both narrative and theatrical.

Sender expounds, on his own terms of course, his personal religious beliefs in *Ensayos sobre el infringimiento cristiano* (*Essays on the Christian Infringement*), 1967, a collection of six essays. By the "Christian infringement," he explains in a prefatory note, he means that the Christian grasp on Total or Absolute Truth is not final; it is only relative, and, therefore, really a kind of "infringement" upon that Absolute Truth. One recognizes the relativism deriving from the Hegelian dialectical approach applied here to religion. The author sees Christianity as having evolved from an earlier, universal worship of the sun; among primitive peoples that celestial body, the origin of warmth and light, was regarded as the generator of life, "Father." In his efforts to establish the universality of certain religious beliefs, practices, and symbols (e.g., the cross), Sender demonstrates his exceptional knowledge of religion as practiced by widely divergent peoples in both ancient and modern times. Jesus is seen not as the historical Jesus of the Bible, but as a myth created through the centuries by the collective unconscious of mankind; as such, he is the highest creation of man himself, and, therefore, worthy of our worship, writes Don Ramón. *Essays* has to date received little, if any, critical attention; it is an authoritative source for those interested in Sender's unique religious outlook.

In *Tres ejemplos de amor y una teoría* (*Three Examples of Love and a Theory*), 1969, Sender examines the amorous relationships of three great novelists and their lovers: Balzac and Madame Hanska, Tolstoi and Sofía Andreievna, Goethe and Carlota. After the first chapter, entitled "Before Beginning," he devotes an anecdotic chapter to each pair of lovers followed by a chapter of highly personal and intuitive commentary on the sex-love relationship previously narrated. In the case of Balzac and Madame Hanska, the abundant correspondence between the two principals is the source for the narrative chapter; for Tolstoi and Sofía Andreievna, Goethe and Carlota, fiction and factual material (from diaries) are judiciously mixed. The final chapter, following the story of Goethe and Carlota, consists not so much of specific commentary on Goethe (as revealed in the novel, *Werther*) as it does of a criticism of the tendency in Spanish middle-class Catholic society to view sex as "bad" (since it is matter, i.e., rooted in natural instincts), and love as "good" (since it is spirit, i.e., an idealization or "spiritualization" of relations between man and woman). Most of this seventh chapter is an abridged and revised version of the author's *Letter from Moscow on Love* published thirty-five years earlier. The book is an unusual combination of narrative and expository matter.

Eighteen of Sender's essays which had formerly appeared in various periodicals and newspapers throughout the Western Hemisphere form the contents of *Ensayos del otro mundo* (*Essays from the Other World*), a handsome volume published in 1970 by Destino in Barcelona. Ranging in subject from a discussion of "hippies" in American society to observations on pre-Columbian Indians, from a chapter on "The Miseries and Grandeurs of Traveling" to penetrating appraisals of Bertrand Russell, Somerset Maugham, D. H. Lawrence, or comments on the latest book or books that the author has happened to read, these essays reveal Sender as a man of prodigious culture and experience who has supremely mastered the art of writing "only interesting things." The book makes available to Spaniards a selected sample of the rich contents of the more than five hundred articles which Sender has published as a syndicated semi-monthly literary column in Hispanic-American newspapers since 1950.

CHAPTER 9

Summation

R AMÓN Sender is an original voice in the Spanish fiction of this century, and an established figure in world literature. Though primarily a novelist, he has written substantially in other genres—short story, drama, poetry, essay, and journalistic articles. In fundamental substance and vision his prolific literary work over more than four decades reveals a remarkable unity and consistency. Exploring a few fundamental concepts, Sender has written about them from widely different angles and under a surprising variety of conditions, times, and places. Disdainful of excessive attention to style, he has written much and polished little; consequently, the totality of his production is highly uneven in quality but includes numerous passages which can surely rank with the best Spanish literature of all times.

Since his earliest works Sender has exhibited pronounced philosophical and metaphysical preoccupations, and his writing has served him as a vehicle for ceaseless probing of certain immutable problems of existence, especially the question of death or man's mortality, but also of the enigma of evil in the individual and in the world at large, the struggle of the individual for self-realization and a sense of worth (because he is human), man's desperate need for a transcendent ideal, the search for an ultimate basis for moral judgments, and the function of the mysterious and the nonrational in life (seen as originating in the unconscious). Sender has made a constant effort to comprehend and reflect total or "essential" reality in his work; in such a view, he ever seeks to accommodate both life and death, reason and intuition, "good" and "evil," the "real" and the "unreal," etc. His deep sense of human worth is rooted in his private view of the ultimate nature of reality, a view which has given him a feeling of essential unity with

166

all mankind and has motivated his vital interest in the social and political issues of today; his work has never lost its dimension of quixotic protest against social injustice.

The most distinctive contribution Sender's fiction makes to Spanish and world literature of this century is its peculiar fusion of ordinary or "photographic" realism with fantastic and lyrical-metaphysical dimensions. Ordinary reality is only the necessary supporting base allowing the author to launch incursions (sometimes successful, sometimes unsuccessful) into the realm of the mysterious, the marvelous, and the lyrical-metaphysical. Successful merging of the two "worlds" creates a new twilight "world," pregnant with poetic truth and capable of opening the "eyes" of the reader to new ways of perceiving that mysterious reality we call life. Don Ramón's "realism" is in accord with the generally antirealistic tendency of European literature in recent decades.

In originality and depth of thought and vision, poetic sense, human understanding, breadth of interest, and sheer volume of production, I know of no living Spanish writer who can equal Ramón Sender. As I bring this book to a close it is good to know that his work goes forward. With each new novel this living Don Quixote will strive to write the ideal work—to attain unto an absolute ideal—and each time he will fail. But he will not yield; he must reach again "for the unreachable star," and dream again "the impossible dream."

Notes and References

Preface

1. Marcelino C. Peñuelas, *La obra narrativa de Ramón J. Sender* (Madrid: Gredos, 1971), p. 15. Writes Peñuelas: "I dare to place Sender at the head of Spanish *novelists* of our time.
"In this top position it is usual to place Baroja."

Chapter One

1. Josefa Rivas in Chapter I, "Biografía de Ramón J. Sender a través de su obra," of her book, *El escritor y su senda. Estudio crítico-literario sobre Ramón J. Sender* (México: Mexicanos Unidos, 1967), 340 pp.
2. Ramón J. Sender, *Los cinco libros de Ariadna* (New York: Ibérica, 1957), p. viii.
3. Stanley J. Kunitz and Howard Haycraft, editors, *Twentieth Century Authors* (New York: The H. W. Wilson Co., 1942), p. 1262.
4. *Ibid.*, p. 1263.
5. Rosario Losada Jávega, in 1966, was the first to report correctly *both* the place and the date of Sender's birth. In her unpublished doctoral thesis, accepted at the University of Barcelona, June 23, 1964, "Algunos aspectos de la novela española en la emigración: Ramón J. Sender," she gives 1902 as the year of the author's birth, but in the 24-page abstract of her thesis, published in 1966 at the University of Barcelona, she records the correct date, February 3, 1901.
6. *A Man's Place*; tr. by Oliver La Farge (New York: Duell, Sloan and Pearce, 1940), pp. 3–4. Acknowledgment here must also be made to pages 25–26 of the thesis by R. Losada Jávega, listed in Note 5 above.
7. Antonio Sierra, a lifelong resident of Alcolea who now occupies the home formerly owned by Sender's father, told me in August of 1969 that the author's father owned no farm—at least around Alcolea. Yet in a tape recording, "Living Literature" at the University of Southern California, June 7, 1966, Sender reported that he came from a family of "small, modest landlords." Could he have been

referring to his grandparents? Did his father acquire land after leaving Alcolea in 1911? Is Mr. Sierra mistaken?

8. With the sole exception of Peñuelas who states on page 51 of his book *Conversaciones con Ramón J. Sender* (Madrid: Editorial Magisterio Español, 1970) that Sender *tuvo que ir a terminar el bachiller a Alcañiz (Teruel)*, former biographers have reported that Sender graduated from the Institute of Zaragoza. Peñuelas's statement is ambiguous since Alcañiz and Teruel are separate cities in Southern Aragon, about ninety miles apart.

9. *Arriba* (Madrid), January 21, 1969, p. 2.

10. I am indebted here to Peñuelas (p. 54 of his book, Note 8 above) for the name of the association or syndicate for which Sender's father managed the newspaper, *La Tierra*.

11. In a conversation in Los Angeles on June 11, 1969, Sender told me that he spent only fourteen months in military service during the African campaign, in 1923–1924, and not 1922–1924 as formerly reported, for example, in Peñuelas's brief sketch, page 55 of his book (Note 8 above).

12. Reported by Rosario Losada Jávega in her doctoral thesis, page 30 (Note 5 above).

13. In *Boletín del Instituto de Medicina* (Barcelona), Año V, núm. 49 (Dic. 1963), 9–10, 12–17, 19–20, and 22–23.

14. Rafael Sender, the author's youngest brother who is an engineer-agronomist in Barcelona, told me in August of 1969 that his father died in 1950 in Lérida, capital of the Catalonian province of the same name, where he spent his declining years.

15. Ramón J. Sender, *Orden público* (México: Publicaciones Panamericanas, 1941), p. 38. A reprinting—with some slight changes—of *O.P. (Orden público)* first published in Madrid in 1931 by Cenit, 195 pages.

16. *Ibid.*, p. 140.

17. As reported by Francisco Carrasquer in his book, *"Imán" y la novela histórica de Ramón J. Sender—Primera incursión en el realismo mágico senderiano* (Amsterdam: J. Heijnis, 1968), p. 21. Carrasquer's book includes the most scholarly study of *Imán* thus far published.

18. According to a conversation I had with Sender in Los Angeles, June 11, 1969, although José R. Marra-López reports such collaboration in his book, *Narrativa española fuera de España—1939–1961* (Madrid: Guadarrama, 1963), p. 345.

19. *Counter-Attack in Spain* (Boston: Houghton Mifflin Co., 1937), p. 35.

20. *New York Times*, 13:1, June 10, 1938.

21. Ramón J. Sender, *La Esfera* (Madrid: Aguilar, 1969), p. 21.

This is the definitive edition of *La Esfera* whose first edition was published in Mexico in 1939 as *Proverbio de la muerte*. The author considers it his most serious and ambitious work.

22. Sender, *Los cinco libros de Ariadna*, p. ix (Note 2 above).
23. *Ibid.*, p. viii.

Chapter Two

1. Sender, *Los cinco libros de Ariadna* (New York: Ibérica, 1957), p. ix.
2. Salvador de Madariaga, *Spain* (New York: Creative Age Press, 1943), p. 24.
3. George Tyler Northup, *An Introduction to Spanish Literature* (Chicago, Illinois: University of Chicago Press, 1946), p. 6.
4. *España en síntesis* (Madrid: Servicio Informativo Español, 1971), p. 36.
5. Sender, *Los cinco libros*, p. xiv (Note 1 above).
6. Salvador de Madariaga, *Genius of Spain* (Oxford: Clarendon Press, 1923), p. 32.
7. Martin Lebowitz, "Thought and Sensibility," *Kenyon Review* (Spring, 1943), p. 220.
8. Madariaga, *Spain*, p. 25.
9. Sender, "1947's Biggest Literary Anniversary," *The Saturday Review of Literature*, August 9, 1947, p. 7.
10. In a recording of "Living Literature" at the University of Southern California, dated June 7, 1966.
11. John T. Reid, *Modern Spain and Liberalism* (Stanford, Calif.: Stanford University Press, 1937), p. 3.
12. *España en síntesis*, p. 121 (Note 4 above).
13. *The Frozen Sea* (New York: Oxford University Press, 1948), p. 28.
14. An effective witness to the faith of European intellectuals during the thirties and to their subsequent disillusionment is the book, *The God that Failed*, edited by Richard Crossman (New York: Bantam Books, 1952).
15. Marcelino C. Peñuelas, *Conversaciones con Ramón J. Sender* (Madrid: Magisterio Español, 1970), pp. 93–94.
16. Sherman H. Eoff, *The Modern Spanish Novel* (New York: New York University Press, 1961), p. 234.
17. *Ibid.*, pp. 234–35.
18. A good starting point for an investigation of the influence of French Surrealism upon Sender would be my article, "Surrealism in Two Novels by Sender," *Hispania*, 51:2 (May, 1968), 244–52.

19. Julia Uceda, "Realismo y esencias en Ramón Sender," *Revista de Occidente,* No. 82 (January, 1970), 45.

20. In his book, *Conversaciones con Ramón J. Sender,* p. 38 (Note 15 above).

21. In Introduction to *Narradores de hoy,* edited by Edith Helman and Doris K. Arjona (New York: W. W. Norton and Co., 1966), p. xix.

22. *Ibid.*

23. Peñuelas, *Conversaciones,* p. 268 (Note 15 above).

Chapter Three

1. Francisco Carrasquer, *"Imán" y la novela histórica de Sender* (London: Tamesis Books Limited, 1970), p. 15.

2. *Ibid.,* p. 66.

3. Marcelino C. Peñuelas, *Conversaciones con Ramón J. Sender* (Madrid: Magisterio Español, 1970), p. 115.

4. Rafael Bosch, "La 'Species Poetica' en 'Imán,' " *Hispanófila,* No. 14 (January, 1962), 33–39.

5. Otis Ferguson, "Hell Could Freeze Over," *New Republic* (October 16, 1935), p. 275; and Paul Allen, "Pro Patria," *New York Herald Tribune Books* (October 6, 1935), p. 14.

6. V. S. Pritchett, "New Novels," *New Statesman and Nation* (September 8, 1934), p. 296.

7. Alfred Kazin, "Seven Red Sundays," *New York Herald Tribune Books* (October 11, 1936), p. 10; and Philip Jordan, "Proletarian Novels," *New Statesman and Nation* (May 16, 1936), p. 772.

8. Peñuelas, p. 119 (Note 3 above).

9. *Ibid.,* p. 118.

10. Sender, *Seven Red Sundays* (New York: Liveright Publishing Corporation, 1936). Translated by Sir Peter Chalmers Mitchell.

11. Manuel Béjar, "La personalidad en la novela de Ramón J. Sender," unpublished dissertation at the University of Utah, 1970, p. 104. Béjar's chapter on *Seven Red Sundays* is a penetrating and thoughtful analysis of Sender's "man-person" dichotomy as seen in the conflict between Samar and Amparo. I am indebted to him for some of the ideas I express in this chapter.

12. Leigh White, "Seven Red Sundays," *Nation* (October 24, 1936), p. 499.

13. Kazin, p. 10 (Note 7 above).

14. Theodore Purdy, Jr., "A Novel of the Madrid Anarchists," *Saturday Review of Literature* (September 26, 1936), p. 5.

15. F. T. Marsh, "Revolt in Madrid," *New York Times Book Review* (October 18, 1936), p. 7.

16. Carrasquer, p. 107 (Note 1 above). An excellent and extensive (twenty pages) analysis of *Mr. Witt.*

17. Peñuelas, p. 129 (Note 3 above).

18. Carrasquer, p. 89 (Note 1 above).

19. V. S. Pritchett, "New Novels," *New Statesman and Nation* (April 10, 1937), p. 596.

20. Eugenio G. de Nora, *La novela española contemporánea (1927–1960)*, II, parte 2 (Madrid: Gredos, 1962), 41.

21. Ramón J. Sender, *El Verbo se hizo sexo (Teresa de Jesús)*, (Madrid: Zeus, 1931), 264 pp.

22. Charles F. Olstad writes in his unpublished doctoral thesis, "The Novels of Ramón Sender: Moral Concepts in Development" (University of Wisconsin, 1960, p. 11), that "In a recent letter (July 11, 1960) Sender says that this work [*El Verbo se hizo sexo*] was written when he was fifteen or sixteen years old."

23. Carrasquer, pp. 207–8 (Note 1 above). In Peñuelas's book, *Conversaciones con Ramón J. Sender,* p. 163, Sender is quoted as saying that he considered *El Verbo* "a foolish work of adolescence, a high school exercise," and that it was published without his intention.

24. Sender, *El Verbo*, p. 9.

25. Review by Homero Serís in *Books Abroad*, 6:1 (January, 1932), 22.

26. Sender, *El Verbo*, p. 7.

27. *Ibid.*, p. 8.

28. Ramón J. Sender, *O.P. (Orden público)*, (Madrid: Cenit, 1931, 195 pp.; Mexico: Publicaciones Panamericanas, 1941, 200 pp.).

29. Ramón J. Sender, *O.P. (Orden público)*, (Mexico: Publicaciones Panamericanas, 1941), p. 6. In "Prefacio del Autor."

30. *Ibid.*, p. 14.

31. *Ibid.*, p. 13.

32. *Ibid.*, pp. 5–6.

33. This is what came from my conversation with Sender in Albuquerque, New Mexico, April 24, 1952, and in a personal letter to me, dated October 21, 1951, in which Sender writes that "the best of them [the three books under discussion] is going to appear recast in *El verdugo afable.*"

34. Sender, *O.P.*, p. 18.

35. *Ibid.*, p. 20.

36. *Ibid.*

37. Ramón J. Sender, *Viaje a la aldea del crimen (Documental de Casas Viejas)*, (Madrid: Pueyo, 1934), 205 pp.

38. Ramón J. Sender, *Casas Viejas* (Madrid: Cenit, 1933), 103 pp.

39. Ramón J. Sender, *La noche de las cien cabezas* (*Novela del tiempo en delirio*), (Madrid: Pueyo, 1934), 244 pp.

40. Juan L. Alborg, *Hora actual de la novela española*, II (Madrid: Taurus, 1962), 33.

41. *Ibid.*

Chapter Four

1. Nicholson B. Adams, *The Heritage of Spain* (New York: Henry Holt and Company, 1943), p. 281.

2. Ramón J. Sender, "Breve Noticia" in *El lugar del hombre* (Mexico: Ediciones Quetzal, 1939), p. 13.

3. Sherman H. Eoff, *The Modern Spanish Novel* (New York: New York University Press, 1961), p. 248. A Spanish translation of this book, *El pensamiento moderno y la novela española* was published by Seix Barral in Barcelona in 1965 (273 pp.).

4. Ramón J. Sender, *Crónica del alba*, ed. with Introduction, Notes, and Vocabulary by Florence Hall (New York: Appleton-Century-Crofts, 1946), v–xxi + 231 pp.

5. *Chronicle of Dawn*, tr. by Willard Trask (Garden City, New York: Doubleday, Doran and Co., 1944), pp. 13–14. All quotations are from the translation by Trask.

6. *Ibid.*, p. 7.

7. *Ibid.*, p. 6.

8. *Ibid.*, p. 12.

9. Marjorie Farber, "Childhood of a Spanish Martyr," *New York Times Book Review* (February 20, 1944), p. 4.

10. *Chronicle*, pp. 13–14 (Note 5 above).

11. *Ibid.*, p. 55.

12. *Ibid.*

13. *Ibid.*, p. 56.

14. *Ibid.*, p. 59.

15. *Ibid.*, p. 159.

16. *Ibid.*, p. 161.

17. *Ibid.*

18. *Ibid.*, p. 196.

19. *Ibid.*, p. 201.

20. Bertram D. Wolfe, "Romantic and Heroic Childhood in Spain," *New York Herald Tribune Weekly Book Review* (March 12, 1944), p. 3.

21. José R. Marra-López, *Narrativa española fuera de España— 1939–1961* (Madrid: Ediciones Guadarrama, 1963), p. 356.

22. Sender, *Réquiem por un campesino español* (*Requiem for a Spanish Peasant*). Bilingual edition with translation by Elinor Randall

and Introduction by Mair José Benardete (New York: Las Americas, 1960), p. 123.

23. Doctor of Education thesis, Columbia University, 1962, 270 leaves.

24. From the Introduction to the school edition of *Mosén Millán* by Robert M. Duncan (Boston: D. C. Heath and Co., 1964), p. x. Writes Duncan: "The anticlerical character of a great part of Spanish literature . . . is not found in Sender's novel."

25. Bernice G. Duncan, Review of *Réquiem por un campesino español*, *Books Abroad*, 36:1 (Winter, 1962), 112.

26. Robert M. Duncan, Introduction to *Mosén Millán*, p. x (Note 24 above).

27. Cedric Busette, "Religious Symbolism in Sender's *Mosén Millán*," *Romance Notes*, 2:3 (Spring, 1970), 482–86.

28. Sender, *Réquiem*, p. 123 (Note 22 above).

29. Busette, p. 486 (Note 27 above).

30. Marcelino C. Peñuelas, *La obra narrativa de Ramón J. Sender* (Madrid: Gredos, 1971), p. 143. Peñuelas also states that for the third plane—the atemporal one—the narrative point of view becomes the "impersonal and anonymous one of the ballad." Thus he sees three planes of action and three narrative points of view. I agree, although one might argue that the work as a whole seeks to transcend time and space while the ballad is perhaps only one obvious technique employed to achieve that ideal end.

Chapter Five

1. Diana Lee Morelli, "The Sense of Time in the Fiction of Ramón Sender," unpublished Ph.D. thesis at the University of Washington (October, 1967), p. 242. Dr. Morelli's thesis, in her own words, "undertakes to show that the meaning of time and space in the most important novels of Sender follows the same lines as those expressed by the author in his philosophical novel, *The Sphere*."

2. For a detailed analysis of the changes effected by the author in *Proverbio de la muerte* to produce *La esfera*, see Chapter V of Manuel Béjar's unpublished doctoral thesis, "La personalidad en la novela de Ramón J. Sender," at the University of Utah, 1970.

3. Marcelino C. Peñuelas erroneously states that the text of the definitive Spanish edition of 1969 is identical to "the English editions," on page 195 of his book, *La obra narrativa de Ramón J. Sender* (Madrid: Gredos, 1971).

4. (Madrid: Taurus, 1962), p. 60.

5. *Narrativa española fuera de España—1939–1961* (Madrid: Guadarrama, 1963), p. 387.

6. *New York Times Book Review* (May 1, 1949), p. 6.

7. "This Man Sender," *Books Abroad,* 14:4 (Autumn, 1940), 354.

8. Julian Palley, "*The Sphere* Revisited," *Symposium,* 25:2 (Summer, 1971), 171.

9. (Madrid: Gredos, 1971), pp. 195–214.

10. (Madrid: Magisterio Español, 1969), p. 142.

11. See Chapter IV, "El sistema vitalista 'ganglionar,' " in Béjar's thesis (Note 2 above).

12. Sherman H. Eoff, *The Modern Spanish Novel* (New York: New York University Press, 1961), p. 247.

13. *Ibid.,* p. 237.

14. *Ibid.,* p. 247.

15. *Proverbio de la muerte* (Mexico: Quetzal, 1939), pp. 9–10.

16. Sender, *La esfera* (Madrid: Aguilar, 1969), p. 7.

17. Julia Uceda, "Realismo y esencias en Ramón J. Sender," *Revista de Occidente,* No. 82 (January, 1970), 47.

18. Sender, *Pro Patria* (Boston: Houghton Mifflin, 1935), p. 198.

19. "Literature in the Middle of This Century," *Phi Kappa Phi Journal,* 29 (December, 1949), 25.

20. *The Modern Spanish Novel,* p. 238 (Note 12 above).

21. See "El hombre y su antitético," pp. 196–215 of Béjar's thesis (Note 2 above).

22. Abstract of "El pensamiento religioso de Ramón J. Sender," unpublished Ph.D. thesis at the University of Southern California, 1968, 285 leaves. The quotation here appears in my article, "Ramón J. Sender: Don Quixote Rides Again," in *The American Book Collector,* 20:6 (March–April, 1970), 20.

23. Sender, *Mexicayotl* (Mexico: Quetzal, 1940), p. 249.

24. *Spain* (New York: Creative Age Press, 1943), p. 25.

25. Sender, *El Verbo se hizo sexo (Teresa de Jesús),* (Madrid: Zeus, 1931), p. 145.

26. *The Modern Spanish Novel,* p. 238 (Note 12 above).

27. Personal conversation in Albuquerque, New Mexico, April 23, 1952.

28. "Faustian Germany and Thomas Mann," *New Mexico Quarterly Review,* 19 (Summer, 1949), 200.

29. Sender, *Las criaturas saturnianas* (Barcelona: Destino, 1968), p. 139.

30. Philippians 1:21–23, The New Testament.

31. Sender, "On a Really Austere Aesthetic," *Books Abroad,* 16:2 (Spring, 1942), 122.

32. *Ibid.,* 119–23.

33. Terms used in Sender's novel, *Mr. Witt Among the Rebels*

(Boston: Houghton Mifflin, 1938), 136–37, which I regard as roughly synonymous to the "ganglionic" in Sender's terminology.

34. Marcelino C. Peñuelas, *Conversaciones con Ramón J. Sender* (Madrid: Magisterio Español, 1969), p. 145.

35. *The Modern Spanish Novel*, p. 241 (Note 12 above).

36. In a conversation with Sender in his home in Albuquerque, April 24, 1952, and reported on page 385 of "An Exposition of the Synthetic Philosophy of Ramón J. Sender," my unpublished Ph.D. thesis at the University of Southern California, 1953.

37. Peñuelas, *Conversaciones*, p. 144 (Note 34 above). Peñuelas reports Sender as saying: "Of Jung I have read nothing . . . but I have read Freud, especially his theory of dreams, his theory of the subconscious." But Sender indicates that his ganglionic theory did not originate from his reading of Freud.

38. "The Parabola of Poetry," *View—The Modern Magazine*, Series V, No. 5 (December, 1945), 10.

39. *Ibid.*

40. *Ibid.*

41. Sender, "On a Really Austere Aesthetic," pp. 120–21 (Note 31 above).

42. *Ibid.*, pp. 119–23; and by implication in *Chronicle of Dawn, The Sphere*, and other novels.

43. In Introduction to Ernest Hemingway, *A Farewell to Arms* (New York: The Modern Library, 1932), p. xvii.

44. In Author's Preface to *Crónica del alba*. Edited with Introduction, Notes, and Vocabulary by Florence Hall (New York: Appleton-Century-Crofts, 1946), p. xviii.

45. *The Modern Spanish Novel*, p. 243 (Note 12 above).

46. "*The Sphere* Revisited," p. 178 (Note 8 above).

47. *Ibid.*

Chapter Six

1. "Versions of Documentary," *The Sewanee Review* (Autumn, 1948), pp. 676–77.

2. Of the four books devoted exclusively to Sender only one, *Conversaciones con Ramón J. Sender* by Marcelino C. Peñuelas, gives as much as two pages to *The King and the Queen*. Marra-López in his important book, *Narrativa española fuera de España* (Madrid: Guadarrama, 1963), cites the enthusiastic review of it by Domingo Pérez Minik (*Novelistas españoles de los siglos XIX y XX* [Madrid: Guadarrama, 1957], pp. 302–6). Juan Luis Alborg (*Hora actual de la novela española*, II [Madrid: Taurus, 1962]), devotes almost four pages (49–54) to the novel, calling it "a perfect work because of

the exactness of its rhythm, and the exemplary sobriety of its elements" (49).

3. Sender, *El rey y la reina* (Barcelona: Destino, 1970), 179 pp.

4. Marcelino C. Peñuelas, *Conversaciones con Ramón J. Sender* (Madrid: Magisterio Español, 1970), p. 165. In reply to Peñuelas's question, "There is also a symbol of Spain and Spanish-ness, is there not? The duchess is the ideal, Spain, and the gardener the Spanish people," Sender replied: "In a way. The duchess is traditional Spain. But as for the rest I prefer to leave it to the reader's interpretation."

5. See Note 1 above.

6. Hebrews 11:1, The New Testament.

7. "The Duchess and Her Gardener," *New York Times Book Review* (June 27, 1948), p. 4.

8. "Versions of Documentary," p. 677 (Note 1 above).

Chapter Seven

1. Ramón J. Sender, *Dark Wedding*, tr. by Eleanor Clark (Garden City, N. Y.: Doubleday, Doran and Co.), p. 174.

2. *Ibid.*, pp. 300-301.

3. Mark Schorer, "Outstanding Novels," *Yale Review* (Summer, 1943), p. vi.

4. Sender, *Dark Wedding*, p. 174.

5. *Ibid.*, p. 135.

6. *Ibid.*, p. 103.

7. Ramón J. Sender, *The Affable Hangman*, tr. by anonymous translator (New York: Las Americas, 1963), p. 209.

8. *Ibid.*, p. 210.

9. Hilary Corke, "Nihilism, Anarchy, the Executioner," *The New Republic*, 149:16 (November 30, 1963).

10. James Gray, "Cynic on the Sidelines," *Saturday Review*, 46:22 (September 7, 1963).

11. In Marcelino C. Peñuelas, *Conversaciones con Ramón J. Sender* (Madrid: Editorial Magisterio Español, 1970), p. 128.

12. Josefa Rivas, *El escritor y su senda (Estudio crítico-literario sobre Ramón J. Sender)*, (Mexico: Mexicanos Unidos, 1967), p. 98.

13. Peñuelas, *Conversaciones*, p. 124 (Note 11 above).

14. Rivas, *El escritor*, p. 169 (Note 12 above).

15. José R. Marra-López, *Narrativa española fuera de España— 1939–1961* (Madrid: Guadarrama, 1963), p. 389.

16. Sender, *La luna de los perros* (Barcelona: Destino, 1969), p. 7.

17. Charles Olstad, Review in *Hispania*, 46:2 (May, 1963), 439–40.

18. Rafael Bosch, Review in *Books Abroad*, 37:2 (Spring, 1963), 189.

19. Sender, *Hipogrifo violento* (Mexico: Colección Aquelarre, 1954), p. 9.

20. Peñuelas, *Conversaciones*, p. 162 (Note 11 above).

21. *Enciclopedia Universal Ilustrada*, LIX (Madrid: Espasa-Calpe, 1928), 370.

22. Sender, *La antesala* (Barcelona: Destino, 1971), p. 243.

23. *Ibid.*, p. 237.

24. Francisco Carrasquer, *"Imán" y la novela histórica de Sender* (London: Tamesis Books, 1970). The first edition of this book was Carrasquer's doctoral thesis at the University of Amsterdam, Holland, and was published by the University in 1968.

25. *Ibid.*, p. ix.

26. *Ibid.*, p. 117.

27. Juan Luis Alborg, *Hora actual de la novela española*, II (Madrid: Taurus, 1962), 7.

28. Antonio Tovar, "Dos capítulos para un retrato de Sender," *Cuadernos del Idioma* (Buenos Aires), Año I, núm. 4, abril, 1966, 24.

29. Carrasquer, *"Imán,"* p. 155 (Note 24 above).

30. Sender, *Carolus Rex* (Barcelona: Destino, 1971), p. 7.

31. Sender, *La aventura equinocial [sic] de Lope de Aguirre* (New York: Las Americas, 1964), p. 50.

32. Readers of Ramón del Valle-Inclán's great American novel, *Tirano Banderas*, 1926, will recognize that its ending and that of Sender's *Lope de Aguirre* are closely parallel, yet, as Francisco Carrasquer has pointed out (*"Imán,"* pp. 200–203 [Note 24 above]), the purposes served in each case are different.

Chapter Eight

1. Marcelino C. Peñuelas, *Conversaciones con Ramón J Sender* (Madrid: Magisterio Español, 1970), pp. 105–6.

2. Sender, "Prefacio" to *Mexicayotl* (Mexico, D. F.: Ediciones Quetzal, 1940), p. 9.

3. For the quotation here and below I use the English translation by Florence Sender in Ramón Sender, *Tales of Cíbola* (New York: Las Americas, 1964). The present quotation is taken from page 111.

4. *Ibid.*

5. *Ibid.*, p. 120.

6. Sender, *Cabrerizas Altas* (Mexico: Mexicanos Unidos, 1965), p. 90.

7. The first three stories, "La llave," "La hija del doctor Velasco," and "La fotografía del aniversario," had previously formed the contents of Sender's book, *La llave* (Montevideo: Alfa, 1960; and New York: Las Americas, 1963).

8. According to Joaquín Ortega in "The Editor's Corner," *New Mexico Quarterly* (Spring, 1950), p. 4.

9. *Ibid.*

10. Sender, *La llave* (Montevideo: Alfa, 1960), p. 10.

11. Sender, "La fotografía," *Cuadernos americanos*, Nov.–Dic., 1951, pp. 276–93. In German translation, "The Photograph" has been staged several times in Germany.

12. Sender, *La llave y otras narraciones* (Madrid: Editorial Magisterio, 1967), p. 175.

13. Sender, *Las gallinas de Cervantes y otras narraciones parabólicas* (Mexico: Mexicanos Unidos, 1967), p. 35.

14. Among these short stories are the following in English translation: "Tale from the Pyrenees," *Quarterly Review of Literature*, 1:2 (Winter, 1944), 119; "The Dancing Witch," tr. by Oliver La Farge in *Heart of Europe*, edited by Klaus Mann and Hermann Kasten (New York: L. B. Fischer, 1943), pp. 175–83 (an excerpt from *A Man's Place*); "The Clouds Did Not Pass," *The Pen in Exile*, I, edited by P. Tabori (London: The International Pen Club for Writers in Exile, 1954), 126–33, and in *New Mexico Quarterly*, 27:1–2 (Spring–Summer, 1957), 17–26; "The Old Wetback," *Southwest Review*, 40:4 (Autumn, 1955), 311–22; and "The Black Cat," *Texas Quarterly*, 4:1 (Spring, 1961), 240–48. In Spanish the following stories, among others, have appeared: "El gato negro," *Cuadernos americanos*, 44:2 (marzo–abril de 1949), 268–78; and "Lo mejor que Dios ha hecho: un día después del otro," *Cuadernos* (Paris), 58 (marzo de 1962), 57–62.

15. According to information in "Otras obras del autor," Verso leaf 4, of Ramón J. Sender, *El lugar del hombre* (Mexico: Ediciones Quetzal, 1939).

16. Sender, *El secreto* (Madrid: Ediciones Tensor, 1935), 16 pp.; and in English translation as "The Secret," in *One-Act Play Magazine*, 1 (November, 1937), 612–26, and also in *Drama I*, edited by Marjorie W. Barrows (New York: Macmillan, 1961), pp. 81-98.

17. Sender, *Hernán Cortés* (Mexico: Ediciones Quetzal, 1940), "Noticia," Verso leaf 2.

18. Swain, Review of *Hernán Cortés* in *Books Abroad*, 15:1 (Winter, 1941), 74.

19. Sender, "The House of Lot," *New Mexico Quarterly*, 20:1 (Spring, 1950), 27–40; and "Das Haus von Lot," *Merkur* (Baden-Baden, Germany), December, 1950.

20. Sender, *El diantre* (*Tragicomedia*), (Mexico: De Andrea, 1958); reworked and reprinted as "Comedia del diantre" in *Comedia del diantre y otras dos* (Barcelona: Destino, 1969).

21. Sender, "The Wind," tr. by Elinor Randall, *New Mexico Quarterly*, 33:2 (Summer, 1963), 185–212.

22. This play was originally published in serial form in *La estafeta literaria*, 362, January 28, 1967, pp. 19–22; 363, February 11, 1967, pp. 16–24; and No. 364, February 25, 1967, pp. 17–21.

23. Bosch, " 'The Migratory Images' of Ramón Sender," *Books Abroad*, 37:2 (Spring, 1963), 132. Bosch's six-page article, of course, can only be the beginning place for a more complete study of Sender's excellent poetry.

24. Sender, *Madrid-Moscú* (Madrid: Pueyo, 1934), p. 130.

25. Stowe, "Immortal Saga from Spain," *New York Herald Tribune Books* (November 21, 1937), p. 2.

26. Sender, *Unamuno, Valle-Inclán, Baroja y Santayana* (Mexico: De Andrea, 1955), p. 137.

27. For a thoughtful refutation of Sender's appraisal of Unamuno and his work, one should read "Reminiscence and Interpretation; An Evaluation of Ramón J. Sender's Essay: 'Unamuno, Sombra Fingida,' " by Oscar A. Fasel in *Hispania*, 42:2 (May, 1959), 161–69.

Selected Bibliography

The list below includes all of Sender's books through 1971, except for some which were first published separately but later incorporated by the author into other longer books, in which cases only the later and more definitive works are listed, e.g., the novel *Ariadna* (*Ariadne*), 1955, which later became the first part of *Los cinco libros de Ariadna*, 1957, does not appear, but *Los cinco libros* does. First editions as well as subsequent printings or editions are given; changes in titles appear in brackets. English translations of his books are listed separately.

For more complete information the reader should consult the three bibliographies listed under "Secondary Sources." For entries from periodicals, the following form is used: 34:3 (June, 1964), 184-91. This means volume 34, number 3, date of publication, pages 184 to 191.

PRIMARY SOURCES

1. Novels

Imán (Madrid: Cenit, 1930; Barcelona: Balagué, 1933).

O.P. (*Orden público*) (Madrid: Cenit, 1931; Mexico: Publicaciones Panamericanas, 1941).

El Verbo se hizo sexo (*Teresa de Jesús*) (Madrid: Zeus, 1931).

Siete domingos rojos (Barcelona: Balagué, 1932).

Viaje a la aldea del crimen (*Documental de Casas Viejas*) (Madrid: Pueyo, 1934).

La noche de las cien cabezas; novela del itempo en delirio (Madrid: Pueyo, 1934).

Mr. Witt en el cantón (Madrid: Espasa-Calpe, 1936; Madrid: Alianza Editorial, 1968). Winner of the National Literature Prize in Spain.

El lugar del hombre (Mexico: Quetzal, 1939; [*El lugar de un hombre*] Mexico: CNT, 1958).

Epitalamio del prieto Trinidad (Mexico: Quetzal, 1942; Barcelona: Destino, 1966, 1969).

La esfera (Buenos Aires: Siglo Veinte, 1947; Madrid: Aguilar, 1969).

A greatly augmented and revised version of *Proverbio de la muerte* (Mexico: Quetzal, 1939).

El rey y la reina (Buenos Aires: Jackson, 1949; Barcelona: Destino, 1970).

El verdugo afable (Santiago de Chile: Nascimiento, 1952; Mexico: Aguilar, 1970).

Mosén Millán (Mexico: Aquelarre, 1953; [*Réquiem por un campesino español; Requiem for a Spanish Peasant*] New York: Las Americas, 1960; Buenos Aires: Proyección, 1961, 1966; [*Mosén Millán*] Boston: Heath, 1964).

Bizancio (Mexico: Diana, 1956; Andorra la Vella [Principado de Andorra]: Andorra, 1968).

Los cinco libros de Ariadna (New York: Ibérica, 1957). The first *libro* formerly appeared as a separate novel, *Ariadna* (Mexico: Col. Aquelarre, 1955).

Los laureles de Anselmo (Mexico: Atenea, 1958; Barcelona: Destino, 1971).

La tesis de Nancy (Mexico: Atenea, 1962; Madrid: Magisterio Español, 1968, 1969).

La luna de los perros (New York: Las Americas, 1962; Barcelona: Destino, 1969).

Los tontos de la Concepción (Sandoval, New Mexico: Coronado, 1963).

Carolus Rex (Carlos II el Hechizado) (Mexico: Mexicanos Unidos, 1963; Barcelona: Destino, 1971).

Crónica del alba (New York: Las Americas, 1963 [Vols. I and II]; Barcelona: Delos Aymá, 1965 [Vol. I]; 1966 [Vol. II]; 1966 [Vol. III]; Madrid: Alianza, 1971 [Vols. I, II, and III]). A novel in three volumes and nine parts: Volume I, "Crónica del alba," "Hipogrifo violento," "La quinta Julieta"; Volume II, "El mancebo y los héroes," "La onza del oro," "Los niveles del existir"; and Volume III, "Los términos del presagio," "La orilla donde los locos sonríen," and "La vida comienza ahora." The first part of Volume I was first published in 1942 (Mexico: Nuevo Mundo, 1942), as a separate novel. Its school-text edition (New York: Appleton-Century-Crofts, 1946) has had numerous reprintings and has made it probably Sender's best-known novel in the United States. The remaining two parts of Volume I and the first part of Volume II also originally were issued as separate novels: *Hipogrifo violento* (Mexico: Col. Aquelarre, 1954); *La quinta Julieta* (Mexico: Costa-Amic, 1957); and *El mancebo y los héroes* (Mexico: Atenea, 1960).

La aventura equinocial [*sic*] *de Lope de Aguirre* (New York: Las

Americas, 1964; Madrid: Magisterio Español, 1967). Normal spelling of *equinoccial* used in the 1967 edition.

El bandido adolescente (Barcelona: Destino, 1965).

Tres novelas teresianas (Barcelona: Destino, 1967).

Las criaturas saturnianas (Barcelona: Destino, 1968). Essentially incorporates contents of *Emen hetan,* formerly published as a separate novel (Mexico: Costa-Amic, 1958).

Nocturno de los 14 (Barcelona: Destino, 1969).

En la vida de Ignacio Morel (Barcelona: Planeta, 1969). Winner of the Planeta Prize.

Tánit (Barcelona: Planeta, 1970).

Zu, el ángel anfibio (Barcelona: Planeta, 1970).

La antesala (Barcelona: Destino, 1971).

2. Short Stories

Mexicayotl (Mexico: Quetzal, 1940). Nine fantastic stories from Mexican mythology.

Novelas ejemplares de Cíbola (New York: Las Americas, 1961; Santa Cruz de Tenerife, Canarias: Romerman, 1967). Twelve stories, some with settings in New Mexico.

Cabrerizas Altas (Mexico: Mexicanos Unidos, 1965). Besides "Cabrerizas Altas," contains "El Tonatiu" and "Las rosas de Pasadena."

La llave y otras narraciones (Madrid: Magisterio Español, 1967). Five stories, the first three of which appeared earlier in a collection entitled *La llave* (Montevideo: Alfa, 1960; and New York: Las Americas, 1963).

Las gallinas de Cervantes y otras narraciones parabólicas (Mexico: Mexicanos Unidos, 1967). Four stories.

El extraño señor Photynos y otras novelas americanas (Barcelona: Delos-Aymá, 1968). Five stories, including "Los tontos de la Concepción," formerly published as a novel.

Novelas del otro jueves (Mexico: Aguilar, 1969). Seven stories including "El sosia y los delegados," published separately as a novelette in 1965 (Mexico: Costa-Amic, 1965).

Relatos fronterizos (Mexico: Mexicanos Unidos, 1970; Barcelona: Destino, 1972). Seventeen stories, narrative-essays, and personal commentary.

3. Theater

Hernán Cortés (Mexico: Quetzal, 1940).

Jubileo en el Zócalo (New York: Appleton-Century-Crofts, 1964; Barcelona: Delos-Aymá, 1967).

Comedia del diantre y otras dos (Barcelona: Destino, 1967). Three plays, the first of which was published in 1958 as *El diantre* (Mexico: De Andrea, 1958).

Don Juan en la mancebía (Mexico: Mexicanos Unidos, 1968; Barcelona: Destino, 1972).

4. Poetry

Las imágenes migratorias (Mexico: De Andrea, 1960).

5. Essays and Journalism

El problema religioso en Méjico (Madrid: Cenit, 1928).
Teatro de masas (Valencia: Orto, 1932).
Casas Viejas (Madrid: Cenit, 1933).
Carta de Moscú sobre el amor (Madrid: Pueyo, 1934).
Proclamación de la sonrisa (Madrid: Pueyo, 1934).
Madrid-Moscú (Madrid: Pueyo, 1934).
Contraataque (Madrid-Barcelona: Nuestro Pueblo, 1938).
Examen de ingenios; los noventayochos (New York: Las Americas, 1961). Includes contents—slightly revised—of earlier book, *Unamuno, Baroja, Valle-Inclán y Santayana* (Mexico: De Andrea, 1955), plus new material.
Valle-Inclán y la dificultad de la tragedia (Madrid: Gredos, 1965).
Ensayos sobre el infringimiento cristiano (Mexico: Mexicanos Unidos, 1967).
Ensayos del otro mundo (Barcelona: Destino, 1970).

6. Translations into English

Imán:
Earmarked for Hell. Tr. by James Cleugh (London: Wishart, 1934) and as *Pro Patria* (Boston: Houghton Mifflin, 1935).

Siete domingos rojos:
Seven Red Sundays. Tr. by Peter Chalmers Mitchell (London: Faber and Faber, 1936; New York: Liveright Publishing, 1936; Harmondsworth, Middlesex: Penguin Books, 1938; New York: Crowell-Collier, 1961; New York: Collier Books, 1968).

Mr. Witt en el cantón:
Mr. Witt Among the Rebels. Tr. by Peter Chalmers Mitchell (London: Faber and Faber, 1937; Boston: Houghton Mifflin, 1938).

Contraataque:
The War in Spain. Tr. by Peter Chalmers Mitchell (London: Faber and Faber, 1937) and as *Counter-Attack in Spain* (Boston: Houghton Mifflin, 1937).

El lugar del hombre:
A Man's Place. Tr. by Oliver La Farge (New York: Duell, Sloan and Pearce, 1940; London: Jonathan Cape, 1941).

Epitalamio del prieto Trinidad:
Dark Wedding. Tr. by Eleanor Clark (Garden City, N. Y.: Doubleday, Doran and Co., 1943; London: Grey Walls Press, 1948).

Crónica del alba:
Chronicle of Dawn. Tr. by Willard R. Trask (Garden City, N. Y.: Doubleday, Doran and Co., 1944; London: Jonathan Cape, 1945). Later becomes the first part of the three-part novel, *Before Noon,* listed below.

El rey y la reina:
The King and the Queen. Tr. by Mary Low (London: Grey Walls Press, 1948; New York: The Vanguard Press, 1948; New York: Grosset and Dunlap, 1968). The 1968 edition is in paperback, and has a five-page introduction by Raymond Rosenthal.

La esfera:
The Sphere. Tr. by Felix Giovanelli (New York: Hellman, Williams and Co., 1949; London: Grey Walls Press, 1950).

El verdugo afable:
The Affable Hangman. Tr. by Florence Hall (London: Jonathan Cape, 1954; New York: Las Americas, 1963; London: Redman, 1964).

Crónica del alba, Hipogrifo violento, La quinta Julieta:
Before Noon. Tr. by Willard R. Trask and Florence Hall (Albuquerque: New Mexico University Press, 1958; London: Gollancz, 1959). Volume I of the *Crónica del alba* series.

Mosén Millán:
Requiem for a Spanish Peasant. Tr. by Elinor Randall (New York: Las Americas, 1960). Bilingual edition with parallel texts in Spanish and English.

Novelas ejemplares de Cíbola:
Tales of Cibola. Tr. by Florence Sender, Elinor Randall, Morse Manley, *et al.* (New York: Las Americas, 1964).

SECONDARY SOURCES

1. Bibliographies

DOMENICALI, DENA. "A Bibliography of the Works by and about Ramón José Sender in the English Language," *Bulletin of*

Bibliography, 20:3 (September–December, 1950), 60–63, and 20:4 (January–April, 1951), 93. Helpful annotations.

KING, CHARLES L. "Una Bibliografía Senderiana Española (1928–1967)" ("A Senderian Bibliography in Spanish [1928–1967]"), *Hispania*, 50, Membership Issue (October, 1967), 629–45. Incomplete but very useful. Includes book reviews. Annotated.

————. "A Senderian Bibliography in English, 1950–1968, with an Addendum," *The American Book Collector*, 20:6 (March–April, 1970), 23–29. Annotated. Addendum lists reviews in English of books in Spanish.

2. Books

CARRASQUER, FRANCISCO. *"Imán" y la novela histórica de Ramón J. Sender* (Amsterdam: University of Amsterdam, 1968; [*"Imán" y la novela histórica de Sender*] London: Tamesis Books, Limited, 1970). A very able critique of Sender's historical novels, and an excellent stylistic study of *Imán*. In addition to *Imán*, *Mr. Witt en el cantón, Bizancio, Los tontos da la Concepción, Carolus Rex, La aventura equinoccial de Lope de Aguirre, Tres novelas teresianas,* and *Las criaturas saturnianas* are analyzed.

PEÑUELAS, MARCELINO C. *Conversaciones con Ramón J. Sender* (Madrid: Magisterio Español, 1970). Illuminating insights into Sender's literary production by both Peñuelas and the author.

————. *La obra narrativa de Ramón J. Sender* (Madrid: Gredos, 1971). A stimulating and scholarly treatment of Sender's narrative art with special attention to *Imán, El verdugo afable, Mosén Millán,* and *La esfera*.

RIVAS, JOSEFA. *El escritor y su senda (Estudio crítico-literario sobre Ramón J. Sender)* (Mexico: Mexicanos Unidos, 1967). A doctoral thesis at the University of Valencia which reviews, somewhat superficially, ten novels and two collections of short stories; contains a good chapter on style.

3. Periodical Articles and Essays in Books (Only selected items are listed here, in chronological order.)

LORD, DAVID. "This Man Sender," *Books Abroad*, 14:4 (Autumn, 1940), 352–54. Valuable insights into Sender as a man. First known article in English on the Aragonese author.

KING, CHARLES L. "Sender's 'Spherical' Philosophy," *PMLA*, 69:5 (December, 1954), 993–99. A discussion of Sender's monistic philosophy as it appears in *The Sphere*.

EOFF, SHERMAN H. *The Modern Spanish Novel* (New York: New

York University Press, 1961). A penetrating analysis of the philosophical implications of *The Sphere* and *A Man's Place*.

BOSCH, RAFAEL. "La 'Species Poetica' en 'Imán,'" *Hispanófila*, 14 (January, 1962), 33–39. An illuminating and appreciative study of the poetic dimensions of *Imán*.

ALBORG, JUAN LUIS. *Hora actual de la novela española, II* (Madrid: Taurus, 1962). Devotes 46 pages to a review of 15 narrative works.

MÁRRA-LÓPEZ, JOSÉ R. *Narrativa española fuera de España—1939–1961* (Madrid: Guadarrama, 1963). A rather general and subjective survey of Sender's novelistic work before and after exile.

KING, CHARLES L. "Surrealism in Two Novels by Sender," *Hispania*, 51:2 (May, 1969), 244–51. An attempt to link Sender to the French Surrealist movement by an exposition of main themes in *The Sphere* and *The King and the Queen*.

UCEDA, JULIA. "Realismo y esencias en Ramón Sender," *Revista de Occidente*, 82 (January, 1970), 39–53. A competent analysis of the "essential realism" which Sender seeks to communicate through his works.

PALLEY, JULIAN. "*The Sphere* Revisited," *Symposium*, 25:2 (Summer, 1971), 171–79. Perceptive.

Index

191